HOW TO FIND
THE
LOVE OF YOUR LIFE

Other Books by Ben Dominitz:

TRAVEL FREE! How to Start and Succeed in Your Own Travel Consultant Business (Prima Publishing, 1984).

Quantity discounts are available from Prima Publishing & Communications, Post Office Box 1260, Rocklin, CA 95677-1260; Telephone: (916) 632-4400. On your letterhead, include information concerning the intended use of the books and the number of books you wish to purchase.

HOW TO
FIND THE
LOVE
of Your
LIFE

A Step-by-Step Program That Really Works

Ben Dominitz

PRIMA PUBLISHING

PRIMA PUBLISHING and colophon are registered trademarks of Prima Communications, Inc.

Library of Congress Cataloging-in-Publication Data

Dominitz, Ben.
     How to find the love of your life : a step-by-step program that really works / Ben Dominitz.
        p. cm.
     Bibliography
     Includes index.
     ISBN 1-55958-321-5
     ISBN 0-7615-0839-2
     1. Mate selection. 2. Dating (Social customs)
     3. Intimacy (Psychology). I. Title.
     HQ801.D68 1985
     646.7'7   85-19249
                                               CIP

97 98 99 00 01 02 AA 10 9 8 7 6 5 4 3 2 1
Printed in the United States of America

How to Order
Single copies may be ordered from Prima Publishing, P.O. Box 1260BK, Rocklin, CA 95677; telephone (916) 632-4400. Quantity discounts are also available. On your letterhead, include information concerning the intended use of the books and the number of books you wish to purchase.

Visit us online at http://www.primapublishing.com

To my editor, my motivator, my partner, my best friend, and most of all, the love of my life, Nancy Duncanson Dominitz.

TABLE OF CONTENTS

ACKNOWLEDGMENTS

Writing is a lonely task. It is, therefore, especially appreciated when friends take time to read and critique a manuscript. Under their scrutiny, errors — both obvious and elusive — come to the fore.

I wish to thank the following people for their willingness to read and offer critical comments on the manuscript of *How to Find the Love of Your Life*: Helen Duncanson, Dr. Baxter and Corinne Geeting, Nancy Martinelli-Duggins, Hatley Mason, and Bernice Garson Slater.

My gratitude, also, to Dave Willmon for being a "mensch."

And finally, here's a toast to my wife, Nancy, one of the finest editors I know, for putting up with my less-than-flawless manuscript.

For whatever errors and inaccuracies which may still exist, I take full responsibility.

*...Two people holding each other like
flying buttresses. Two people depending
on each other and babying each other
and defending each other against the
world outside. Sometimes it was worth
all the disadvantages...just to have
that: one friend in an indifferent world.*

Erica Jong

Chapter One

Chance Encounters
and Other Popular Myths

"You must be kidding!" exclaimed Ann, my outspoken seat partner on the flight from Sacramento to Los Angeles, after I told her the title of the book I was writing. "Listen, I've tried everything to meet men — from singles clubs to dance lessons. Last year, I went on a three-day cruise, the kind that promises romance and adventure on the high seas. What a joke! Besides the couples on board, there were 207 women and 89 men on the ship. It wasn't a cruise, it was a meat market. And the guys I did meet were real jerks — you know, the open-shirt and gold-chain-type. I'll never do *that* again!"

Nodding sympathetically, I asked, "And what are you doing now to meet new people?"

"What am I doing?" she asked rhetorically. "Like most of my friends, I try not to think about it too much. I like my work, so I can manage pretty well most of the time. I guess you could say that I mix long periods of inaction with an occasional kamikaze attack on some male." Then, shrugging

3

her shoulders, she added thoughtfully, "What else can I do? I suppose that I cling to the belief that when I meet the right person, I'll know it and he'll know it."

"I wouldn't call myself exactly shy," said Scott, a thirty-five-year-old computer programmer, "but when I get back from work, the last thing I want to do is go to a singles bar and play the same old tired game. Besides — I guess admitting this is not too macho — but I've never enjoyed going to bed with a stranger. And at work, I don't meet too many people. So besides getting together with my friends at the ski club, I spend a lot of time alone."

"If you could find someone who'd make you happy, would you be interested in a permanent relationship?" I asked.

"Sure!" replied Scott eagerly. "Any ideas?"

Ann and Scott are not alone in their frustrations. They are part of a growing number of otherwise productive, well-adjusted men and women of every age, background, and income level who are silently withering inside from loneliness and lack of love.

Unlike those for the unemployed, the government does not keep statistics on the many who desire a permanent relationship and cannot find it. There are no federal programs to help the lonely, no "unattached compensation" or single placement centers. And no one bothered to include loneliness in the infamous misery index used during the Carter administration. No, this one aspect of our pursuit for happiness is left up to us.

Wouldn't it be wonderful if, in our technologically advanced age, a computer program were created that would link and match all the right people with each other? Unfortunately (or fortunately) this is not to be. There is yet to be a test devised that can predict the compatibility and

4

mutual attraction of two people (which is why computer dating, once the rage, has lost much credibility). Over eighty years after Freud's theories shook the world of psychology, our knowledge of what makes people mutually attractive and compatible is, at best, patchy. Besides, would you really want a machine to make this major life decision for you? No, my friend, the task of finding our mates will and, I believe, should always be left up to you and me.

The Numbers Game

Recently, a number of books and articles have appeared on the subject of "how to find a mate." Some of them offer excellent advice on various aspects of the male/female game. Others are merely exploitive. Some concentrate on how to meet men (unlike this book, which is written for both genders, most are addressed to women only) while others tell you how to get a man to fall in love with you. But universally, these books and articles fail to offer a viable, step-by-step strategy, one which shows those who are ready to take charge of their search how to go about finding the love of their life. Instead, what they do offer are more variations on "the numbers game."

The numbers game theory exists in every field, from sales and job hunting to finding love. It is a popular theory, one that is seductive in its simplicity. It goes like this: If you circulate and meet enough people of the opposite sex (from now on known as POS), you will eventually find your mate. Therefore, the way to find a love partner is to go anywhere and everywhere that single people abound.

Does this work? Do people meet others at parties and art gallery openings or by walking their poodle, cat, or pet mongoose? Of course they do. *Sometimes*. People do meet others in all kinds of places. Do they find *compatible mates* by pursuing the numbers game? Not very often — but often enough to create the stuff of which legends are made. When Lorna, the secretary on the other side of the office building, gets married to someone she met on the dance floor of a singles' night spot, everyone learns about it. And all the five hundred singles in the building are newly infused with the hope that maybe they, too, will bump into their perfect mate under the strobe lights. And thus, they are lulled back into their hopeful complacency.

The truth is that for most people, starting a conversation with a complete stranger is quite traumatic. It's especially difficult if they feel that they have an ulterior motive for their "spontaneity." As Gunther, a forty-two-year-old engineer from San Francisco, confided, "Whenever I go out with the idea of meeting a woman, I feel unnatural. I hate trying to think of things to say to a perfect stranger. Besides, I don't know anything about her background, like whether she's married or involved with anyone else. Sometimes I really get discouraged."

Unfortunately, the publicity generated by an occasional success in meeting a stranger and having that blossom into a permanent relationship far exceeds the frequency with which it happens. People simply do not talk about their failures. Patti is not about to tell you about the man she met in a singles bar who, she discovered the following morning, was married. Nor is James likely to advertise how the woman he met at the art auction spent the next hour haranguing about sexism and the innate rottenness of all men.

Lack of Intimacy

The challenge in developing satisfying relationships, however, goes far beyond that of simply making initial contact with strangers. There still lies a huge chasm between the process of meeting POS and that of developing real intimacy.

In their book, *Pairing*, George R. Bach and Ronald M. Deutsch (see Bibliography) describe poignantly the consequences of the numbers game:

> By the millions, men and women yearn for intimate love and cannot find it — not knowing how easily intimacy can be experienced, how effectively the emptiness can be filled.
>
> Some are truly alone. And night after night, day after day, they stalk one another, at once both the hunters and the hunted. They prowl the singles bars and clubs and hotels and cruises and weekend trips. They haunt church socials and civic meetings, office water coolers and public tennis courts, the ski slopes and the beaches and the charter flights to Europe.
>
> Robed and groomed and scented for the ritual, the brasher ones reach out, and the quiet ones watch and dream and wait. Then, with rare exceptions, everyone goes home, if not empty-handed at least empty-hearted, feeling a little more lonely, a little more hopeless — chilled in contrast with the warmth of communion they sought and did not find.

All of us, at one time or another, have experienced the destructive elements of the mating game. Especially for sensitive people, it is a loathsome ritual. The fear of rejection, the dating of incompatible people, the awkward, artificial conversations, the why-did-I-ever-go-out-with-him/her feeling afterwards — all come with the territory. We have wasted precious time with people who were not suitable and, in the process, have become discouraged.

What's wrong? Why has the process of getting to know our counterparts become such a traumatic experience? Haven't we gone through the sexual revolution, presumably, to remove the barriers between the sexes? Why is it that after spending an evening (or a night) with a person of the opposite sex (POS), we end up knowing so little about him or her?

Perhaps the best visual imagery of the loneliness many experience is the way people dance. For more than twenty-five years now, people have been dancing *at* each other, gyrating their bodies independently of their partners' actions, intensely ensconced in their own world. There is no intimacy. People don't touch each other, they just occupy the same space for a short while. (As of this writing, there seems to be emerging a new and welcome trend. According to society band leader Peter Duchin, as reported in *New York* magazine, "Touch dancing is coming back now among young people and old people, and it's not nostalgia. It's getting away from the more narcissistic . . . kind of dancing by yourself. It's the desire to be close to somebody.")

There are real similarities between the contemporary don't-touch-me type of dancing and the typical first date. We may spend an evening together, but instead of getting to know the total human being we go through a tiresome ritual. Talking at each other without really listening, we devote our time trying to impress one another. "Dazzle the other person" is one of the favorite games we play in order to erect a protective wall around ourselves. Presumably, if we impress our dates enough, they won't find out how scared and lonely we really are. This usually backfires. Our oft-rehearsed self-portrait of invulnerable perfection intimidates our dating partners into feeling inadequate — a mirror of our own fears and insecurities.

Often, on the basis of such a superficial first encounter, men and women decide whether or not they like each other and if they are compatible enough to continue a relationship. Not the most satisfactory route to closeness, wouldn't you agree? And yet, this ritual is as pervasive today as it has ever been.

Don't misunderstand me. I'm certainly not attacking the institution of dating. It is and will remain a fun, often romantic, and even necessary way for people to court each other. But as a means of *beginning* a new relationship, the first date, with all its tension and stressful superficiality, tends to encourage game-playing instead of honest communication.

The problem of achieving meaningful communication between strangers is real. Unfortunately, the masks people wear when meeting others for the first time are so set in place that, too often, the real persons behind them are never discovered.

The Rejection Factor

One of the biggest flaws with the numbers game theory is that it inevitably leads to inaction. Why? Because most people have a limit to the amount of rejection they can take. In the numbers game, singles are supposed to walk up to perfect strangers and initiate conversation. Don't get me wrong, I, too, believe in encouraging people to be as open and assertive as possible. However, the reality is that after a few rebuffs or embarrassing moments, all but the most persistent souls become discouraged. As Claire, a thirty-three-year-old guitar teacher, confided, "I still go out to meet men, but every time it doesn't work out, it takes me weeks to get up the courage to try again."

It may be lamentable, but most people do internalize their unsuccessful efforts. They come to see failed attempts as personal rejections. What's worse, they blame themselves for their difficulties. Among those I interviewed, I met many who interpreted their loneliness as a sign of inadequacy. This feeling only reinforced further a growing sense of futility concerning their chances for a relationship. As a result of this what's-the-use-of-trying attitude, millions of bright, capable, and giving men and women opt to spend their evenings in front of their TV sets, too discouraged to persist in their search for the companionship and love they crave, need, and deserve. This is a tragedy of immense proportions.

The Chance Encounter Myth

When people are confronted with a too-bleak reality, they resort to hoping instead of doing. When that happens, they often fall prey to the "chance encounter" myth. The chance encounter is one of the most addictive emotional narcotics around. Like the Cinderella fantasy, it promotes the belief that if one waits long enough, the perfect person will simply come along. For these chance-encounter "junkies," the idea of employing a plan to meet suitable POS seems abhorrent. After all, they might argue, love ought to be romantic. If one used a method or a plan to meet others, wouldn't that take away from the romance, the spontaneity? This idea that a chance encounter is really the way it ought to happen is understandable. The fantasy is powerful, almost irresistible. . .

> . . . The strains of "Some Enchanted Evening" are heard in the background . . .

> Out of nowhere, he appears . . . the tall, dark, immensely rich stranger with the defiant mane of a

10

wild stallion. His nostrils flare as he surveys the
room. Suddenly, his piercing blue eyes fix their gaze
on me. I tremble as I feel his presence penetrating my
inner being. His warm smile tells me that in this one
instant he understands that I am the warm, perceptive,
passionate, intelligent, desirable, understanding, mag-
nificent woman he has long searched for . . .

There is nothing wrong with fantasy. Fantasies help us all
keep our sanity by offering occasional escape from the
mundane. But what makes fantasies such a wonderful
release? It's precisely because they *are* an escape from the
realities of every day that make them so appealing. Harlequin
Romances and the stories of Rosemary Rogers are simply
not the way it is for most of us. Our personal suffering
increases when we seriously expect the chance encounter to
provide us with a suitable partner.

Sounds ridiculous, doesn't it, to expect a suitable mate to
enter our lives and announce his/her presence? And yet, the
vast majority of single people must believe in this fantasy, at
least some of the time. I say this because none of the singles I
interviewed answered in the affirmative when pressed with
the question, "Do you have a clearly defined plan to meet
suitable people of the opposite sex?"

And here is the crux of the matter. Most of us leave the
process of finding our mates to the whims of destiny. Or
perhaps we expect an overworked God to find one for us.
Super-achievers, men and women who would never dream of
leaving their career progress to chance, become timid
children when it comes to the mating ritual. Indeed, I have
met bright, intelligent, vibrant, and otherwise assertive
people, who, when it comes to selecting a person with whom
they would want a relationship, become passive and
unimaginative — wallflowers, waiting in vain to be picked.

As I write this, I can already anticipate the letters I'll receive from those who are happy with their singlehood. They will protest that I paint a much-too-bleak picture of the unattached state. Further, they will tell me how happy they are being unencumbered by any serious relationships. I realize that there are those who prefer a life of solitude. And if that's the lifestyle that works best for you, that's grand. This book is not written for those who enjoy being single. It is written for the *reluctant* unattached who have realized that *for them*, having a mate is an essential ingredient for happiness.

A Word to Women

It's hard to escape it! It is the subject of many articles and columns to the lovelorn. Books have been written about it. On every talk show or discussion on the subject of finding love, one statistic is being repeated: There are somewhere between seven to nine million more women than men at the marriageable age. These are ominous numbers, ones that can understandably intimidate any woman seeking a permanent relationship. Indeed, according to one famed psychologist, today's unmarried women should just learn to accept less-than-ideal partners if they want to find companionship. After all, how can you ever hope to beat the odds, right?

Forgive me if I bristle at what I consider to be the condescension that some display toward the unattached individual. Smugly, married "experts," from the Olympian security of their marital state, advise the unmarried to "settle for less." And instead of solid information, singles are offered the tyranny of statistics (how can anyone argue against cold, hard facts?) while being exhorted to "circulate and meet more people," as if they didn't know that.

That's the problem with statistics. Used incorrectly, they are dehumanizing and demotivating. They can give you the feeling that you are just a number with no control over your life, so why bother to try? If you are a man, at least theoretically, you've got it made. (Do you hear that, Scott and Gunther?) And if you are a woman, unless you look like Raquel Welch, you'd better succumb to a life of loneliness or else settle for what you can get.

The apparent shortage of men can be compared to the job market during an economic downturn. Even in a recession, at a time when there are more people looking for jobs than there are jobs, those who know what they want and how to find it fare considerably better than those who just wait for conditions to change. In fact, millions of people do find employment even during a recession, just as a record number of marriages are occurring and untold millions of close non-marital relationships are forming all the time.

Sometimes the victims of loneliness perpetuate their own self-defeating propaganda. I recently overheard a conversation among a group of single women. They were discussing men and how hard it is to find "good ones." Since the conversation took place at a busy lunch spot, I instinctively glanced around me. I saw at least four men having lunch alone. It amazed me to think that here was this small enclave of women talking about the dearth of men when, in reality, they were surrounded by several "possibilities." Why hadn't it occurred to them to simply invite the men to join them? Is it possible they were focusing more on the problem than on the solution? The truth is that while there *are* more single women than men who are unattached, there are, nevertheless, millions of guys who are lonely, who hate singles bars and other "marketplaces," and who don't have the slightest clue as to how to go about meeting a compatible mate.

And there is even more good news. Each day, new men become eligible for new relationships. They include those who immigrate to America or those who migrate to your town. Then there are those who terminate old relationships and those who reach a point when they are ready for permanent pairing. But ultimately, the main reason you are likely to succeed is because, unlike you, most singles are not involved in a *campaign* to find the love of their life. Even the vast majority of those who are actively seeking relationships approach the whole process in a haphazard, hit-or-miss manner. In addition, when one considers that there are uncounted millions who, for one reason or another, have given up hope altogether and have stopped searching, mere statistics become meaningless.

So don't let the statistics and the harbingers of bad tidings discourage you. *You* have the power within you to create the conditions for a love relationship if you really want to. That is what this book is about.

Am I giving you a pep talk? You bet I am! Isn't it time someone did? And here is some more good news. (Now I'm beginning to feel like Paul Harvey.) In a recent issue of *Los Angeles*, the city's own magazine, the personal classifieds listed twenty-seven ads by women and thirty-five by men. Even allowing for the fact that men, traditionally, are expected to be more aggressive, I found these figures significant. Instead of stressing "fun and games," many of the ads placed by men emphasized the desire for a long-lasting relationship. Think about it! Some of these ads were written by attorneys, professors, physicians, and other professionals who resorted to using the classifieds in order to meet suitable POS. In other words, *they are not meeting compatible women on their own!* With a campaign designed to put you in touch with the "hidden" POS, you will reach men like these who are, just like you, searching. For the more

14

mathematically-minded among you, here is another way to look at your prospects for success. Even if only one out of two singles will succeed in finding a mate (these numbers are hypothetical) and if you become four times more effective in making a quality contact with suitable POS than most unattached people, your chances of finding a permanent relationship are dramatically improved.

No, my friend, there are no magical formulas that guarantee instant success. But there *are* millions of single men out there, many of whom would enjoy meeting *you*. And when you are the one working through the steps of an effective campaign to meet them, you are much more likely to achieve your objective than the majority who passively wait for their "chance encounter."

Focus the Picture

Another reason why so many do not have a clear idea of where to begin their search is because they don't know what they're looking for. No matter how desperate you might feel (and I do hope that you are not), it's not good enough to say, "If he wears pants and can fog up a mirror, he'll do." Or, as one woman was overheard saying, "I used to look for a knight on a horse. Now, I'd settle for the horse."

As amusing as these stories are, they underline a major problem. Many singles, both men and women, vacillate back and forth between unrealistically high expectations of the qualities a mate must possess and no standards at all. On the one side, parental indoctrination and teenage fantasies result in the search for a mate so perfect that he or she could not possibly exist. On the other side, need and even desperation remove discretion. This kind of wild fluctuation in behavior is counterproductive to one's chances for finding a lasting relationship.

Where We Go from Here

As you read further, you will discover an exciting program filled with ideas to help you find "that special someone." But of all the thoughts presented in this book, the most important is this: *You need never again be a victim of the mate-selection process. Instead, you can be in complete charge, guiding and directing your campaign with total confidence until you reach your desired goal of finding the love of your life.*

This, in a nutshell, is the premise of the book. You *can* and *should* be in control of finding a mate, which is, after all, one of the fundamental ingredients to your happiness. And why shouldn't you take control? You have taken charge of many other areas of your life, haven't you? Now, with the modest guidance of this book, you can conduct your own campaign to end your life of singlehood and begin a wonderful, new, flourishing relationship.

You are going to discover that the ideas and techniques are presented in a clear, logical way. And from the beginning, you should be aware of the book's contents. The following is a listing of those main ideas:

1. You are more likely to find a suitable POS if you make up your mind that you really do prefer a permanent relationship over singlehood.

2. You are more likely to find a suitable POS if you are willing to make a commitment to go on a high-priority campaign to find him or her.

3. You are more likely to find a suitable POS if you know the kind of person that you would find appealing.

16

4. You are more likely to find a suitable POS if you know what major strengths and attributes you'll be bringing to a relationship.

5. You are more likely to find a suitable POS if you learn how to be almost irresistibly attractive whether or not you are naturally endowed with physical beauty.

6. You are more likely to find a suitable POS if you make up your mind that you are "window shopping," not desperately trying to force a relationship to happen.

7. You are more likely to find a suitable POS if you develop a campaign that will allow your friends, relatives, and acquaintances to lead you to a variety of POS in a dignified, fun way.

8. You are more likely to find a suitable POS if you learn how to use referrals and referral interviews to reach exciting new people.

9. You are more likely to find a suitable POS if you learn how to meet POS in ways that remove stress and artificiality that are a part of most first dates.

10. You are more likely to find a suitable POS if you learn how to communicate with POS in ways that allow both of you to develop intimacy and trust.

11. You are more likely to find a suitable POS if you always deal from a position of strength, by not having all your "eggs" in one "relationship basket," thus allowing you to retain your independence and leave your options open.

This is the gist of the book. The following chapters evolve from these ideas and offer you appropriate suggestions and techniques. It's going to be a fun journey together. Shall we get started?

Chapter Two

There's Gotta Be a Better Way

How to Find the Love of Your Life was written in order to give you a viable alternative to the numbers game and the chance encounter. Here, you'll discover a method that will show you that, indeed, it's possible for you to meet, face-to-face, one-to-one, as many eligible, compatible people of the opposite sex as you wish to meet. Instead of having to face the potential for an unpleasant encounter with a total stranger with whom you may have little in common, you'll enjoy meeting qualified prospects, people who are also eager to meet you. Furthermore, if you are willing to commit yourself to following the steps outlined here, you will be in a position to create more friendships and possible love relationships than you've ever imagined.

Where do these ideas come from? As we begin our relationship (and I hope, friendship) with each other, I want to share with you a bit of the origins of this book.

For a period of twelve years, I had been involved in consulting people in the area of sales and entrepreneurship. One of my chief responsibilities was the training of several thousand sales people in innovative methods of creating new business contacts. This meant that almost daily I had to deal with individuals, many of whom had been shy and awkward in speaking to anyone, and infuse them with the knowledge and confidence to talk with people they had never met before. During this period of time, I witnessed near miracles of personal growth accomplished by men and women whose only asset was a genuine desire to get ahead. What was remarkable to see was how this new-found confidence transferred itself to almost every other area of these individuals' lives. With coaching and encouragement, those who had once been inhibited became downright adventurous in their willingness to talk to others. I treasure the victories of those who overcame their fears among my most gratifying experiences.

In addition, because of some work I performed in the field of career counseling, I was privileged to learn, in depth, some of the most successful methods involved in helping people find their ideal career. One of the fundamental ideas behind successful job hunting is that the best jobs are usually hidden from the majority of job hunters and career changers. In fact, a successful career search consists largely of uncovering this hidden job market — positions that are not advertised in the classifieds or listed in the personnel departments of companies.

While I was busily involved in the career field, a friend called and asked to see me. She had been a former student of my sales training and was now a successful entrepreneur in our city. When we met, she seemed a bit anxious and fidgety. In fact, her impatience grew with each passing minute of our preliminary chitchat. Finally, I asked why she wanted to see me. It was then that she told me that a year earlier she and her husband had divorced and that she was now looking forward to meeting eligible men. I still didn't understand what it was she wanted me to do. Finally, she said, "Ben, you once helped me hone my sales skills. Now I need your advice in another area. How do I meet the kind of men with whom I could develop a long-term relationship?"

To say the least, I was flabbergasted. Here was a successful woman in her early forties — good-looking, intelligent, self-confident, affluent — who was having difficulty meeting compatible men. Not knowing what to say, I took the easy way out by asking her to give me a couple of weeks to think about the matter.

Over the next few days, I couldn't get this unusual request out of my mind. In fact, for reasons I did not yet understand, I became obsessed with it. My initial amazement at my friend's dilemma gradually turned to understanding. Here was a busy professional who was involved daily in the running of her business. Although she knew hundreds of people, her everyday contacts were limited to business relationships. With the added responsibilities of raising two teenage children, it became clear why she would be frustrated in her search for someone special.

Then it hit me — why I found myself so interested in my friend's problem. Instead of staying outside the issue, I began to visualize myself as a single adult. I asked myself the question, "What would I do if I found myself suddenly single?" Although I am fortunate to have a wonderful marriage, I understand that life carries no guarantees. "What if something happened to Nancy — would I know what to do?" I asked myself. Not being the kind of person who would enjoy living alone, I knew how unhappy I would be without someone with whom I could share my life. Like many, I met my spouse while attending college, surely one of the best social laboratories there is. But as a single adult in a predominantly married world, if I were faced with the need to find a permanent mate, would I know where to turn? Because I am certainly not the party-and-singles-bar type, I knew that door would remain closed. And because I tend to become immersed in my work, it would be very much out of character for me to abandon my projects in order to concentrate on my social life. All at once, I realized that, potentially, I could find myself just as lonely and bewildered as my friend.

My friend's situation, which seemed so remote just a few days before, had now become painfully real. I could feel the specter of loneliness starting to haunt me. It occurred to me that this is not just a singles' dilemma, but that even those who are presently married might, one day — through either death or divorce — be confronted with the task of "starting over." It became clear that searching for permanent love in adulthood could be a lonely and even frightening experience. In many ways, it's like hunting for the proverbial needle in a haystack.

Instinctively, I felt there had to be a solution to my friend's problem, that there had to be a better way for finding someone special than just relying on fate or a chance encounter. As I continued to ponder this, I began to see a direct correlation between the experience of looking for a suitable mate and that of finding the right job. In career counseling, I was encountering successful people who were at a loss when it came to searching for the right occupation. And here, a bright single person appeared to be overwhelmed by the apparent difficulty of finding a partner for a serious relationship. (Coincidentally, success in career and success in love are the two main ingredients for the often-elusive recipe for a fulfilling life.) In both cases, people were bewildered as to what to do next.

It is now common knowledge that there are extremely effective ways for men and women to conduct a successful job-hunting campaign. These are described definitively in such books as *What Color Is Your Parachute?* (see Bibliography). But when it comes to the equally important task of finding the ideal mate, there is no evidence of any clearly defined methods having been formulated. (Later, I spoke with a psychotherapist who told me that patients' loneliness is one of the most common problems he and his colleagues encounter. When I asked him what advice was being given, he replied, "We all know the problem. But none of us has any real solutions. I'm afraid that we can do little more than offer sympathy and understanding.")

Almost in spite of myself, I became more involved than I had originally planned to be. Intrigued, I decided to examine the career-search techniques closely to see if they could, just perhaps, be applied to finding the perfect mate. And indeed, I discovered many similarities. Let's take a look at some of these similarities in the chart below:

Finding the Perfect Job	**Finding the Love of Your Life**
1. Identify your assets, abilities and interests.	1. Identify your uniqueness. (Who am I? What makes me special? What do I have to offer?)
2. Identify the qualities a job must have to make you happy (type of work, salary, working conditions, opportunity for advancement, etc.).	2. Identify the qualities that are really important to you in a potential mate. (What's negotiable and what's non-negotiable?)

23

3. Learn how to discover the hidden job opportunities. (The best jobs are rarely advertised.)

3. Learn how to discover the "hidden" POS. (The "best" singles are not necessarily on every street corner.)

4. Meet with people who can put you in contact with the decision-maker who can hire you.

4. Meet with people who can put you in contact with compatible POS.

5. Meet with the decision-maker for a job interview.

5. Meet with a POS for a "non-date" (a relaxed, one-to-one get-together with a "prospect" over a cup of coffee).

As you can see from the comparison above — in both job hunting and in seeking a mate — specific steps must be taken in order to discover the "hidden opportunity." But there the similarities end. In the search for love, when two people meet, it becomes a brand new ball game. The rules suddenly change. It is then up to the two individuals to determine if they like each other well enough to pursue a romantic relationship.

Suddenly, as a result of trying to help a friend, I became aware that I had inadvertently stumbled upon something enormously important. Here was a method of helping not just one person, but many, take charge of a vital area of their lives — one that had previously been left to chance. I became excited when I realized that with enough persistence and by applying the tried-and-true techniques of successful career placement, any man or woman seeking permanent love could avoid years of aloneness. And furthermore, he/she would not have to settle for someone who isn't compatible!

"But how will all this be accepted?" I wondered, knowing that this rational approach to finding a mate would chafe against ingrained notions about romantic love. I could already hear my critics exclaim, "Okay, so looking for a mate resembles finding a job. But what about romance? What in the world does this have to do with falling in love?" Absolutely nothing! But falling in love can only happen *after* two people meet and only *after* they have had a chance to get to know each other. (In spite of the chance-encounter fantasy, people rarely fall in love at the moment their eyes meet from the opposite sides of a crowded room.) The steps described here will simply allow you to become acquainted with a large number of POS in an intimate, one-to-one manner. You can then select one or several with whom you'll be able to develop genuine rapport and mutual attraction.

A full month after I promised to call my friend, I finally reached her. Now, instead of stale advice, I could offer her something real and tangible: a full-fledged campaign that would put her in touch with many unmarried men — men who would have otherwise remained unknown to her. Her initial enthusiasm for my proposal abated somewhat when it became clear that a serious campaign would require a commitment of time, effort, and much persistence. However, after thinking for a moment, her eyes brightened as she said to me, "Okay, I'm ready. I'd rather be busy for a few weeks and pay the price in one lump sum, so to speak, than spend the next few years paying the price of loneliness on the installment plan." It was at that moment that I understood why my friend had established a successful business career. This was obviously no wimp. Here was a woman who was willing to accept the price that must be paid for achieving something of value.

The results of her campaign were hardly miraculous. First,

she didn't get started right away. The typical businessperson, she kept placing other projects on a higher priority. Finally, she did put forth effort, but then only for a period of forty-five days. During that time, however, she managed to have an initial get-together with ten men, go out with six of them, and develop real rapport with two. (All of this will become clear to you as you read, later on, a step-by-step description of the campaign.) For the next two months, she dated both of the men she liked, eventually forming a real bond with one — a forty-seven-year-old divorced physician. At this writing, their relationship seems to be gaining momentum.

Whether my friend settles on this particular relationship or another is beside the point. What *is* important is that she has learned a simple, easy-to-duplicate method to meet as many eligible POS as she wishes, thus gaining control over her chances for a permanent relationship.

This experience only whetted my appetite to learn more about the process of pairing. Infused with enthusiasm and hungry for more information, I decided to research the subject further. I plunged into scores of books and articles on this and related subjects. Indeed, some hinted at the connection between career-seeking and finding a mate. But regrettably, none carried the analogy to its logical conclusion.

Next, I made a point of interviewing numerous single people of both genders. I asked questions and took notes. What struck me most was that many communicated frustration, even self-blame, as a result of their inability to find a suitable mate. It was almost as though they felt like outcasts in their own society — incomplete people in a couples' world.

When I explained my method, the response was, at first, skeptical. But the more information I offered, the more the initial doubt began to dissipate. In fact, there soon appeared an air of exuberance. In one of the sessions, Joanne, a divorced free-lance photographer in her thirties, said to me, "I never thought of finding a mate as something that involves a campaign, but I have to say it does make sense. Besides, it's a little like going on a diet. I can do almost anything for a ninety-day period, especially since the reward could last a lifetime."

Shortly afterwards, I decided that this book *must* be written. It's offered to you with the hope that you, too, will use its principles to gain control over your search for the love of your life.

An Old-Fashioned Idea

Among the foundations on which this method is built is the principle that most people feel much more at ease interacting with those who are familiar to them than with those who are complete strangers. In fact, a portion of your campaign will involve creating referrals that will allow you to meet a new person as a "friend of a friend" instead of as a stranger.

Is this a new idea? Far from it! As part of my research, I began to explore the history of courtship. It soon became apparent that my so-called innovative method of creating a network of new contacts through referrals and introductions was, in actuality, one of the ways men and women had always met each other. This is especially true since in many cultures talking to strangers was frowned upon, particularly for women. For example, if a woman had wanted to meet a man, she would have had to arrange for a mutual friend to introduce them. Was this custom formal and stiff? Perhaps, at least from our vantage point. Nevertheless, this ritual was rooted in the valid idea that if a friend introduced you to someone, he or she had somehow "pre-screened" that person, and, therefore, that individual carried a stamp of approval.

Another old-fashioned ritual this method resurrects is the idea of having friends, acquaintances, and even relatives help you with your search. Prior to the 1930s, before the Great Depression forced millions to uproot themselves in search of employment, most people didn't have to worry about such things as the numbers game and chance encounters. As Vance Packard writes in *The Sexual Wilderness* (see Bibliography), "Until quite recent decades, the U.S. girl tended to fall in love with the boy she had grown up with. He lived within a mile or so of her. Their folks knew each other . . . " Most people lived in the same community as their family and friends and pretty much knew everyone around. They attended the same church and met other single people of similar socio-economic backgrounds in community-organized socials and dances. When someone was shy or widowed, neighbors and relatives would try to introduce them to eligible POS. Often, the whole community would offer a helping hand. The local pastor or rabbi would be on the lookout for potential husbands and wives at nearby congregations, neighbors would introduce their distant cousins to the unmarried folks of the community, and local merchants would offer a running commentary on the new citizens in the area and, naturally, their marital status. In fact, in some of these communities remaining single would have been a terrific feat of independence. As you can see, under those circumstances, most individuals did not have to make decisions about getting married. Marriage just happened at a reasonable period of time after one reached adulthood. Moreover, most marriages lasted a lifetime. No wonder that, aside from the coy rituals of courtship, there was no need to develop skills in finding a husband or wife.

Today, in sharp contrast, many are uprooted from their place of birth. Modern executives and their families expect to be moved several times during the course of their careers, college graduates pursue the best job offers wherever they might be, and retirees move to points south. A different world indeed!

Not only is the geographical isolation from one's roots creating estrangement and loneliness, but fewer than half the marriages today last a lifetime. Is it any wonder, then, that millions of men and women are feeling discouraged at the prospect of finding "the right one?"

As a result of this growing isolation, single people need to develop their own support system for meeting compatible mates. This book will show you how to do this by having you elicit the aid of everyone you know in your search. The good news is that you will be able to get lots of help without your giving up one iota of your dignity. (You might, however, need to rid yourself of some false pride.)

In short, the method that has evolved from the need of one individual, far from being original, simply weds three seemingly disparate ideas into a cohesive whole. By combining the best of the past with modern techniques of sales and career counseling, a method has been created (or perhaps it would be more correct to say collated) that can help *you* be in control of finding the love of your life.

Why 90 Days?

When I discuss the context of this book with others, the question of the ninety-day time frame is often raised. There are two questions that are often asked:

- Why have a time frame at all?
- Why ninety days as opposed to thirty days or twelve months?

One of the things drummed into me during my experience in business was the power of goal setting. Most people become more focused and productive if they have a specific time frame within which they must reach a goal. When we have a clearly defined purpose and a finite time period in which to accomplish it, we become much more efficient than we would be otherwise. We even begin to view all our actions and priorities in relation to our objective.

The power of goal setting works in your life as it does in mine. Indulge me as I offer you a personal example. At this very moment, as I write these words, it is nearly midnight. Since I am innately lazy, I would normally not be sitting in front of my word processor at this late hour. In fact, I can think of at least one nocturnal activity that is much more enticing than the production of a cacophony of clicks on a keyboard. Nevertheless, here I am, punching my way through yet another sentence. Why? For no other reason than the fact that I set a goal to finish this section tonight. And although I am tired and hungry (anyone got a violin?), I have become a slave to my commitment. Such is the power of goal setting.

Another reason why a time frame is important is that it allows you to pace yourself. For instance, if you know that you have ninety days to achieve your goal of finding someone special, you can plan on how many POS you'll want to meet on a daily, weekly, and monthly basis. On the other hand, without a time frame, you may fall into the trap of whiling away your days in procrastination, ambling directionless in spite of your desire for intimacy.

While this explains the reason for having a time frame, it still does not answer the question: Why ninety days? By now, you have probably noticed that I have used the word, "campaign," to describe the process you will go through to find the love of your life. According to my trusty *Webster's New World Dictionary*, Second College Edition, "campaign" is defined as "a series of organized, planned actions for a particular purpose." (It also defines it as "a series of military operations with a particular objective in a war." I suppose that this, too, is appropriate.) This is precisely what you'll be doing: You will work through an exact set of steps for the purpose of meeting suitable POS. By definition, all campaigns have a time frame, and ninety days is more than enough time to meet lots of eligible POS, as long as you take the steps involved. In addition, ninety days is as long as most of us can concentrate on one specific purpose. (Even the Presidential campaign in the United States begins in August and ends with the elections in November.) In short, while no one but a fool or a charlatan can offer guarantees, I am certain that launching and following through with your campaign for the next ninety days will yield you a bounty of POS out of which you'll have the enviable task of having to pick and choose. Ah, yes, to the victor go the spoils!

You are now confronted with a choice. On the one hand, you have the option of luxuriating in the warm, comfortable habits of your past, so familiar and yet so ineffective in producing the kind of relationship you want. Or, you can make the decision to take the next step, which is to learn from this book fresh approaches that will open the door to a new and abundant world of eligible POS.

Is it worth the hassle to go on a ninety-day campaign to find the love of your life? You bet it is! Your happiness is worth it. After all, you are seeking a solution to a central issue, one that affects every part of your being for the rest of your life. For now, all you have to do is read on, absorb the ideas, do the recommended exercises, and follow the simple guidelines. In the next chapter, you'll learn how to remove some persistent obstacles that may be standing in your way of finding love.

Chapter Three

Removing the Obstacles

Anyone who embarks on the search for his or her ideal mate risks disappointment. There's no escaping it. Whenever we attempt a new relationship, we face the possibility of failure. Once a love affair or a marriage dies, feelings of pain and rejection surface. We blame ourselves for this "failure," even as we blame the other person. Invariably, a history of failed attempts can cause us to feel afraid. Thus, when an opportunity for a new relationship arises, instead of openness and enthusiasm, we become ambivalent and timid, reluctant to try again.

In his brilliant book, *Release Your Brakes* (see Bibliography), Jim Newman relates how most of us live our lives like people who drive their cars with one foot on the accelerator and the other foot on the brake. We try to move forward and, at the same time, put a halt on our ability to succeed. Why? Because revolving inside us are conflicting emotions — contradictory feelings which stop us from living and functioning fully.

A great deal has been written recently on the many ways people sabotage their own success. While it is true that most of us have certain built-in resistances or "hang-ups," it can be dangerous to over-emphasize those tendencies. I rather think that, instead, most people are not fully aware of how the mind functions. They tend, therefore, to underestimate their ability to control their emotions and to direct their actions.

In this chapter, we will explore together the obstacles you may encounter and with which you must deal before successfully embarking on your journey to find the love of your life. But simply identifying the roadblocks is not enough. You will also learn how to remove them from your path so that you can succeed in your campaign. This will be discussed under the following headings:

    I.   The Power of Visualization

    II.   The Principle of Vacuum

    III.   Singlehood vs. a Permanent Relationship

    IV.   Overcoming the Fear of Rejection

    V.   Making a Commitment

★ ★ ★

The Power of Visualization

In my early years, I had an experience which clearly demonstrated to me the power of our thoughts over our destiny. At the time, I was struggling to build a business. Things were not going well. At the end of each month, finding money to pay the bills became my primary preoccupation. Over a period of time, I became adept at "robbing Peter to pay Paul." This game of survival lasted for quite a few months. And although I never enjoyed it, I became quite good at it.

Even though I was juggling funds in this mad form of "creative banking," I desperately wanted to succeed and to prosper. And yet, my business was not growing. One evening, the end of the month fast approaching, I found myself once again devising new and inventive ways to pay my bills. Suddenly, it all began to make sense — why my business wasn't succeeding and why each month was such a financial struggle: Instead of planning and carrying forth with a solid plan for growth, I had been focusing all my energy on avoiding disaster. Thinking survival had become an ingrained habit. And although I didn't like my circumstances, they were like an old and tattered bathrobe, a familiar though homely part of my life. The amazing thing is that as much as I wanted it, my chances for success were nil as long as my mind was visualizing ways to "hang in there." As of that night, I consciously devoted time to creating mental pictures which focused on growth rather than mere survival. Gradually, my actions began to change. Instead of simply remaining in the trenches, fighting a battle of everyday existence, I began to plan and act in a way that anticipated success. I no longer allowed myself to think poor. Instead, I began to see myself as "temporarily broke and on the way up." That fateful night marked the beginning of my success in business.

Does this personal anecdote relate to any aspect of your life? Just as I did, you really want to change an important part of your present reality. You have a tremendous desire to, at last, find someone with whom you can share an ongoing, nurturing relationship. And yet, your thoughts may be in conflict with your desires. Ask yourself these questions: What do I think about most — am I simply coping with my present situation as a person living alone, or am I positively planning my future with someone special? Do I think of myself as *permanently* single or as *temporarily* not involved with someone? The difference between these two attitudes will have a great deal to do with your success in finding the love of your life.

Our subconscious mind is very obedient. As Maxwell Maltz, author of *Psychocybernetics* (see Bibliography), explains, it works on creating whatever it is we imagine. That's because the subconscious mind cannot tell the difference between a real event and one that's vividly imagined.

Are you a bit skeptical about the power of your thoughts? Then let's try this simple experiment: Imagine that you have just opened your refrigerator. Your eyes focus on a plump, juicy lemon. You pick it up and hold it in the palm of your hand. It's ice-cold to the touch. Taking a sharp knife, you slice the fleshy, sun-yellow fruit in half. As the knife cuts through it, fragrant juices spurt forth from its center. Breathing in the delightfully pungent yet familiar aroma, you grab hold of one of the halves and place it directly in front of your mouth. You are parched with thirst. Instinctively, you tilt your head upward, and, as you open wide your mouth, your fingers slowly begin squeezing the citric droplets onto your outstretched tongue. Your taste buds are assaulted as you swish the liquid tartness back and forth, back and forth. Ooooh . . . the sourness!

Are your lips puckering? Are your salivary glands working furiously? Good, so are mine! The point is made. The subconscious mind cannot tell the difference between a real event (actually eating a lemon) and one which is vividly imagined (visualizing eating a lemon). I repeat this statement because within it lies a most fundamental and powerful truth: To a large degree, you and I control the direction of our lives by the kinds of mental pictures we create. Just as in the above exercise, our bodies respond to a thought. Sickness/health, success/failure, happiness/unhappiness — all are controlled by the kinds of visualizations we choose. As a result, if the mind is filled with worry and thoughts of impending disaster, the body responds by feeling ill; the mind begins to prepare for the doom that is envisioned. On the other hand, if we create clear pictures of positive expectation, the mind works toward the creation of results that are based on those visualizations. In other words, the mind creates its own self-fulfilling prophecy.

Think of your stream of thoughts as a strong current of water. If those thoughts about relationships are predominantly negative, causing your mind to believe that your present lack of meaningful involvement with someone special is a permanent situation, you would be swimming against the current each time you attempt closeness with anyone. Your mind will sabotage your chances for success because you have programmed it to think that you will be forever alone. On the other hand, if your stream of thoughts is filled with the expectation that something wonderful is about to happen — that *you* are destined for the joyousness that deep love can bring — then your subconscious mind will work *with* you to find creative solutions to your temporary aloneness.

Mark, a thirty-seven-year-old pharmaceutical salesman,

desperately wants to meet a person he can marry. But every time he thinks about going out with someone new, his mind runs the same old "movie." The title? *Past Rejections and Embarrassing Moments.* When Mark met Clarice, a quiet but friendly bank employee who lives in the same apartment complex, he somehow mustered all his strength to ask her out. The date was, as you can well imagine, disastrous. Filled with negative images of impending failure, Mark was so self-conscious that he spent the entire evening over-compensating for his fears. He talked much too much, was totally oblivious to Clarice's feelings, and not once allowed his innate warmth and sense of humor to surface. "I knew it wouldn't work," he consoled himself after Clarice failed to respond positively to his anxiety-filled behavior. What a shame! Especially because Mark and Clarice, both eager for love and intimacy, might have had a chance to develop a real relationship. Yet, the plot was predictable; this depressing scenario was created in Mark's mind long before the date took place.

Had Mark learned to spend time creating clearly defined mental pictures of success, he could have written a new script for the "movie." By visualizing himself having a relaxed, enjoyable evening with Clarice, he might well be on his way to experiencing the pleasures of a budding relationship. Even if Clarice turned out not to be "the one," he could, with real effort, gradually learn to alter his mode of thinking by replacing the painful memories of his past failures with confident expectancy and enthusiasm about meeting women.

What about *your* thoughts? The same principle of visualization and projection is working, right now, in your personal life. Think about it for a moment. Do you spend a lot of time dwelling on your loneliness; or do you see, in your mind's eye, your meeting new and fascinating POS? Do you occasionally blame others, such as your ex-spouse, your parents, your children, or "circumstances" for your present situation; or have you let bygones be bygones so that you can once again eagerly look forward to the future? Are you carrying inside you a rage against all men or all women, seeing yourself as a victim of a conspiracy against your gender by the opposite sex; or do you see each person as, primarily, an individual, never allowing yourself to prejudge? Do you dwell on the fear of never finding your mate, of spending the rest of your life alone; or do you see yourself as a *temporarily* single person who is on an exciting adventure to find the right POS? In short, is your stream of thoughts positive or negative? Are you swimming with the current or against it?

The principle of positive visualization is vital to your success. Make sure that the thoughts and mental pictures you create are consistent with your search for the love of your life.

The Principle of Vacuum
(Uncluttering the Mind)

Are you a busy person? If you are like most of us, your life is probably filled to the brim with duties, activities, and tasks that seem never-ending. You don't know where the time goes (you *do* know that it "flies"), and life seems an endless carousel of activities, to-do lists, and responsibilities. Between work and home and taking care of children, pets, or both, there is little or no time for much else, right?

The world in which we live today is like a three-ring circus. Do you remember going to the circus when you were a kid?

It was so exciting because there were so many things to watch — the clowns, the animals, the acrobats. Today, we experience the same kind of sensory overload on a daily basis. Not only are our lives overflowing with obligations, we also have at our fingertips an inexhaustible supply of recreational distractions. Television brings us world events and mindless escapism. Radio protects us from silence, even in the privacy of our cars. And newspapers and magazines inform us daily of all kinds of disasters and other current events. We are constantly bombarded with visual and auditory clutter — mental pollution. Result? Unless we make a concerted effort to reduce the distractions and focus our lives on clearly defined goals, we can remain inundated with the "junk mail" of life, never focusing on what is really important to us.

Social Clutter

Another stumbling block that can sabotage your chances for success is "social clutter." Often, people begin to form associations and friendships based on their specific needs at a particular time. Later, when those needs change, these same people hold on to relationships that are not only outworn but which may be, in fact, counterproductive. In your campaign to find love and intimacy with a POS, there are three kinds of relationships that, unless you are careful, can actually sabotage your chances for finding the love of your life. Let me illustrate them with the following vignettes:

1. Becoming attached to a married person.

Joyce is the personal secretary to the vice-president of a medium-sized corporation. Jack, her married boss, has become very dependent on her. Although there is no liaison between them, Joyce often works late for him. She also fantasizes about the possibility of becoming romantically involved with Jack.

As long as Joyce focuses on this futile relationship, acting as an "office wife," she automatically closes herself to the possibility of any kind of fruitful relationship with another man. People who behave this way are caught in a web of unrealistic expectations that invite unhappiness. Typically, they are also the people who say, "Why do these things always happen to me?"

2. Belonging to a circle of singles of the same sex.

Janet, like many other single women, has developed a group of friends with whom she shares her joys and disappointments. This has been a wonderfully supportive group. Recently, however, she is feeling that the group is settling into an attitude of benign acceptance of singlehood. Janet is beginning to feel subtle pressure, even propaganda, against anyone going out with men. ("Who needs them, anyway?") It's as though the other women have developed a vested interest in keeping the group intact. Any romantic entanglement by any of the members, therefore, threatens the status quo.

It is wise to analyze your present friendships in light of your goals. Since you are now ready for a special relationship, ask yourself this, "Is my present social life conducive to finding a suitable mate?" If the answer is "No," make the necessary changes that will allow you to achieve your goal — yes, even if this means creating more of a distance between you and some of your current friends.

41

3. Staying with an unsatisfying relationship until "something better comes along."

Cliff has been living with Rosemary for six months. He doesn't love Rosemary and is eager to find someone special. But instead of terminating his present situation, Cliff, who doesn't like to be alone, has rationalized that he should keep things going the way they are until someone more desirable comes along.

As long as Cliff is involved with Rosemary, it's going to be very difficult for him to find someone else. Moreover, he is being unfair to her because of the dishonest premise of their relationship. Cliff needs to put an end to his ambivalence and clear his life of a non-productive bond before he can even begin to think seriously about finding someone special.

Prioritizing Your Life

Just wishing things to be different is not enough to activate change. You must visualize your wants and focus your attention on them, thus removing all unnecessary clutter from your mind. Is finding the right POS really important to you? Then make it one of the top priorities in your life. First, you need to write down those priorities in the order of their importance. Since the idea of devising this kind of list has never even occurred to most people, the chances are that you, too, will need to take some time to create one.

Where would you put finding and interacting with POS on your list of priorities? Obviously, if you have nothing else to do that's important, it can rank at the top of your list. However, most of us lead more complicated lives than that. We have career and family responsibilities that, usually, must take precedence over other things. Still, if finding the love of your life falls within the top four positions (example:

spiritual values, family obligations, job/career, searching for your ideal mate), then you are in an excellent position to succeed in your quest. Now, when the possibility of distraction occurs, all you need do is review your list and ask: "Will my doing this lead to the achievement of my goal, or is it important to any of my top priorities?" If the answer is "Yes," do it. If the answer is "No," don't do it.

Singlehood vs. a Permanent Relationship

Another potential obstacle to developing a permanent bonding with someone is the conflict many singles experience between their longing for a serious relationship and their enjoyment of their independence.

Helen, a successful businesswoman in her mid-fifties, is an example of the ambivalence many singles feel about developing a permanent relationship. Now divorced after many years of taking care of both family and business, Helen finds herself enjoying the peace and quiet that her single status provides her. "It's so nice to come home, put on my robe, pop something into the oven, and curl up with a good book rather than have to cater to someone else," Helen confided. And yet, during another conversation, Helen told me how much she misses the warmth and intimacy of a permanent relationship. "I suppose what I really want is someone to come live with me on the weekends and then have him go to his own place for the rest of the week," she admitted.

This ambivalence on Helen's part is actively interfering with her ability to find a suitable mate. As is the case with many singles, there is the conflict between the advantages of singlehood and the desire for a permanent relationship. The mind, then, receives a jumbled message: a definite maybe. Confusion sets in (one foot on the accelerator and the other foot on the brake). The result: an unclear message to oneself and to a potential mate, which results in inaction and indecision.

This conflict is even more pronounced with those who have never been married. These singles are so entrenched in their own way of life that they often experience great difficulty in visualizing themselves in a permanent relationship. Mary, a never-before-married thirty-three-year-old, claims that she has always wanted to get married. Yet, upon closer examination, she admitted how much she fears relinquishing the total control she now has over her life. As a result, she elects to go out with men who are "friends" but with whom she could never become emotionally or romantically involved.

Indeed, there are valid reasons why many keep vacillating between their preference for their single state and their desire for marriage. Especially if there are no children at home, being single has many advantages. "I go to bed at night with a cat and books and newspapers, and I wake up in the morning with a face full of cat hair and papers all over the bed, only sometimes saying, 'Why am I alone?'" writes Amanda Spake, a Washington-based career woman, in *MS.* magazine. The independence, the freedom of not having to answer to anyone, to come home whenever you wish, to live however you want — these are real advantages. That's why one of the first steps you should take toward finding the love of your life is to resolve your conflict between your present single state and that of seeking a permanent relationship. Make no mistake about it, entering into a long-term union involves making adjustments. Are you prepared to make them? If not, you may not be ready to take on the campaign of finding your mate. So take time to clarify your values. The exercises at the end of this chapter are meant to help you do just that.

Overcoming the Fear of Rejection

Valerie is about to begin her nightly ritual. She is coming home from her job at a major publishing house where she has faithfully served as assistant to the editor for the past five years. She enters her apartment with arms embracing two grocery bags filled with Le Menu frozen dinners for herself; cans of Alpo gourmet dog food for Gatsby, her Great Dane; and a copy of the *New York Times.*

While "preparing" dinner for the two of them, Valerie is thinking about the predictable plot of her nightly activities. After taking Gatsby for his evening walk, she is looking forward to climbing into her old bathrobe, pouring herself a glass of sherry, settling in to read the *Times,* watching "Sisters," and catching up on some extra paperwork she brought home from the office.

It's been five weeks since Valerie has been on a date. And even that one had been arranged by a friend. Having gone through the trauma of divorce a year earlier, Valerie is having difficulty in handling her feelings of rejection. Her prescription has been to avoid risking a relationship altogether. "Maybe my life isn't really what I want it to be," she rationalizes, "but at least it's familiar. Besides, the kind of man I'm looking for doesn't exist, anyway. And if he did, he probably wouldn't be interested in me."

In one way or another, most people internalize the negative impact that comes from the fear of rejection. They interpret this rejection as a personal affront, thus allowing it to shake the basic foundation of their self-image. They even begin to question their innate worth and lovability. That's unfortunate, because to live is to experience rejection. No one is immune from it. Consequently, those who try to shield themselves from further rejection spend more and more

45

energy trying to avoid it altogether. That's when negative visualization in the form of worry and anxiety rears its destructive head. "What if I go on stage and make a fool of myself?" asks the inexperienced community-theater actress before opening night. "All these people seem so sophisticated. What if they find out that I never went to college?" questions the newly divorced plumber invited to a party at a business club. "I get so nervous on the first date. What if she wants to go to bed and I can't perform?" wonders the recently widowed father of two. In each of these examples, negative projections of future events interfere with the possibility of enjoyment and success.

The fear of rejection is our primary block to happiness. It decreases our chances for growth by preventing us from risking new experiences and seeking new relationships. Notice how anxiety-free most young children are. They live one moment at a time and are always eager to try new things. As we grow older, we begin to internalize our negative experiences until we look for safety from them. In a way, being "old" can be measured by how much emotional safety we seek at the expense of emotional growth. Growth requires risk, and risk can cause the pain of rejection.

People handle rejection in various ways at different times. Tom is a newly divorced man with two children whose wife left him for another. For two years he questioned his own self-worth while mourning a relationship upon which he depended for a very long time. Until he completed the process of accepting what happened without blaming himself, his fragile self-esteem could not risk any more rejection. Finally, through the help of a sensitive therapist and by developing new areas of meaning in his life, Tom began to realize his innate value as a man. Now that he knows he is still a worthwhile person with much to offer, he is dating women again. "I'm still afraid of being rejected, but now I'm willing to risk pain for the potential gain."

Mary handles her fear of rejection differently. She goes out with numerous men, indiscriminately. She has learned the technique of emotional detachment. "I learned not to give a damn," she says. "As long as we just have a good time, that's fine with me. But if I see a man getting serious, that's my cue to exit."

Creative Avoidance

One of the most common techniques for not facing rejection is called "creative avoidance." When our minds want to avoid confronting an unpleasant task, we create reasons to be busy. For example, Linda's friend has just given her the phone number of Stewart, a single man who recently moved to her city. She would really enjoy meeting him. Her mind, however, is visualizing thoughts of potential embarrassment and rejection. (What if he feels I'm too forward? Suppose he has someone else in mind? Maybe he won't like the fact that I have children.) As Linda is mustering the strength to call, a girlfriend telephones. Like a thirsty wanderer reaching an oasis, Linda plunges into a long conversation with her friend, conveniently "forgetting" all about Stewart until later that evening . . . when it's "much too late to call."

The degree to which the fear of rejection affects our lives is directly related to the way we view ourselves in relation to others. What adult has never heard a four-year-old exclaim to him, "I don't like you anymore!"? Yet, as mature people, we take this kind of rejection lightly, perhaps even with an indulgent smile. What's the difference? How can we handle this kind of rejection with so much ease and, figuratively, fall to pieces when an adult, especially a POS, expresses the same sentiment?

The answer lies in how we view ourselves. Most of us, as

47

mature adults, see ourselves as more fully formed than young children. Consequently, when a tot rejects us, our self-image tolerates this well because we are not threatened by him. On the other hand, many adults tend to view others as superior. They suffer from the if-you-really-knew-me-you-wouldn't-like-me syndrome. Therefore, when they interpret an event as a rejection, they tend to use this feeling as a confirmation of their negative self-appraisal.

At one time, I went through a period when I, too, didn't feel I measured up. In my early days in business, I would find myself intimidated by people who were financially more successful. Somehow, I felt that they were more worthy than I. "Why would they want to bother with me?" I would question. My solution was to create a scenario in my mind that would allow me to view those individuals on equal footing. I was then able to muster enough courage to contact them. This is what I did: When calling a successful businessman, I visualized his answering the phone in his long johns, sporting a four-day beard, and reeking of halitosis. Instead of feeling anxious, I had to suppress my laughter at a mental picture of someone who appeared so ridiculous. Try this sometime when you are intimidated by calling a POS. It works!

Are you suffering from a low self-image? Do you sometimes have the feeling that the whole world is in on something that you are missing? If so, you are entertaining thoughts that are debilitating and false. Once you accept that all human beings must deal with the universal problems of aging and death, you will realize how fragile we all are. Movie stars, heads of state, and yes, even physicians, all share with you the same desire for a bit of happiness, companionship, and love. Once you accept this, you need never be afraid of being rejected by another fallible and, therefore, vulnerable mortal.

Five Steps to Overcoming the Fear of Rejection

How, then, does one overcome the fear of rejection? Here are some of the ways in which you can tackle this enemy to your happiness:

1. Learn to bring your fear down to size. One very effective way is to confront rejection. Ask yourself this: "What is the worst that will happen if someone says 'No'? Will I still be alive? Will I still have the use of my mind and faculties?" Of course you will! Although no one likes rejection, it is a manageable part of life. You can handle it!

2. Develop a risk/reward mentality. When confronted with an opportunity, successful people ask themselves: "What is the potential reward for my taking advantage of this new opportunity?" Then they ask: "What's the potential risk?" In the case of finding a lasting relationship, your greatest risk is not doing anything. Don't you agree that the potential reward of finding someone with whom you can share your life is worth risking a little rejection?

3. Develop a sense of positive expectancy about risking new relationships. Once you ask yourself what's the worst that can happen and assess the risk/reward factor, concentrate your attention on developing a positive expectancy about your meeting POS. Project clear mental pictures of successful encounters and visualize with enthusiasm POS who are absolutely delighted to meet you.

49

4. Increase your self-esteem. Many people believe that our self-esteem is a constant, that it is either on a high level or a low level. Actually, we all experience fluctuations with our self-image. Predictably, when things go our way, we feel good about ourselves, but when circumstances go against us, our self-esteem falters. It is precisely because of these fluctuations that we can, over a period of time, learn to intentionally uplift our self-concept.

One clue as to how to go about changing our self-esteem comes from new studies on how self-image is formed in the first place. Many psychologists used to believe that our early environment dictates how we view ourselves. However, experiments have pointed out that twins living in the same home and treated the same way can feel different about their relationship with their parents. Each interprets the parents' actions toward him/her in a uniquely personal way. In other words, how we translate the behavior of others toward us dictates how we feel about ourselves. Put another way: "I am not what I think I am. I am not what you think I am. I am what I think *you* think I am."

How does this abstract concept apply to your interaction with POS? Here's an example: Joan has a date with Bill. Bill is supposed to pick Joan up at 8:00. It is now 8:15 and there is no sign of Bill. Joan has a choice. She could think, "I bet he's going to stand me up. That so-and-so, who does he think he is? I'll show him . . . !" Or, she could think, "It's only 8:15. Perhaps he got lost. I'll just relax until he either calls or shows up."

In the first example, Joan, preparing herself for rejection, begins a defensive tirade against Bill. Interpreting Bill's lateness as a put-down, Joan is already feeling victimized. And even if Bill does show up, what kind of an evening do you think they would have?

In the second example, Joan is emotionally in control. She doesn't bother to second-guess what happened to Bill, knowing that she doesn't have the facts at hand anyway. As a result, her self-esteem is intact. She does not make Bill's lateness (his problem) a test of her own self-worth.

Guard against interpreting other people's actions as attempts to victimize you. This is an infantile attitude which clearly shows that you're too self-absorbed for your own good. When you think about it, most people have a hard enough time dealing with their own problems to spend time plotting against you or thinking bad thoughts about you. If their behavior is inconsiderate, it's usually because they are not coping very well. Or maybe they're just boors. Either way, it's their problem. Don't make it yours.

5. View others in the proper perspective. We have covered this point earlier. Do not think of others as superior to you. If you accept all men and women as mere humans — fallible, vulnerable, and potentially lovable — their actions will not have undue influence on you. Even if you feel that someone rejected you, you don't have to feel devastated. Instead, you can walk away with your dignity intact, remembering that he or she is a mere mortal, not a god.

Making a Commitment

There is a story about the chicken and the pig who were taking a Sunday morning stroll. They soon passed a church filled with happy people singing hymns. The chicken, inspired by the music, turned to the pig and said, "Let's do something special for these wonderful people. Why don't we make them a ham and egg breakfast?" The pig was silent for a moment before he answered, "My friend, that's all right for you. You'll simply be making a token donation. But for me, that would be *total commitment!*"

Let me put this as plainly as I can. What this book is about is helping *you* find your perfect mate — someone with whom you can share your life. Aside from food and shelter, and for many, enjoying a fulfilling career, finding a love relationship is perhaps the most significant ingredient for one's happiness. We are talking about your life — your establishing a permanent union with a special person. Remember, you have finally determined that this is vital to your sense of completeness. It may even be the most important task before you right now. So do not be surprised if it's going to take time and effort. It will. To make this project work for you will take real commitment on your part. For the next three months, focus your energies on finding the love of your life. Make it one of your top priorities.

One of the most critical principles of any worthwhile goal is that of making a commitment. Once a commitment is made without the option of backing out, the mind releases tremendous energy toward its achievement. Couple this with clear visualization of exactly what it is you want, and you suddenly unleash tremendous energy toward the accomplishment of that goal. Because of this important principle, I now want you to do something that you might be reluctant to do — something that you may very well construe as being silly — but do it anyway. I want you to sign a contract with yourself, one which states that you are ready to take the plunge and that, for the next ninety days, you are going to make a major effort to use this book as an aid in finding the right person for you. Are you not yet ready to make this commitment? If that's the case, go ahead and read further, and when you are ready to "go for it," turn back to this page and make your pledge.

My Commitment

I, _____ ,
DO HEREBY ACKNOWLEDGE THAT I HAVE MADE THE COMMITMENT TO USE THE PRINCIPLES IN THIS BOOK TO AID ME IN FINDING THE LOVE OF MY LIFE. I SHALL DO THIS FOR A PERIOD OF NO LESS THAN NINETY (90) DAYS.
I FURTHER ACKNOWLEDGE THAT, OTHER THAN MY EMPLOYMENT, FAMILY, AND SPIRITUAL OBLI-GATIONS, I HAVE PUT THIS PROJECT AT THE TOP OF MY PRIORITY LIST.

I REALIZE THAT I MIGHT BE DISCOURAGED ALONG THE WAY BUT THAT MY DESIRE FOR HAPPINESS IS GREATER THAN ANY TEMPORARY SETBACK. I ALSO UNDERSTAND THAT, DURING THIS NINETY DAYS, I WILL PROBABLY FIND ONE OR MORE SUITABLE MATES BUT THAT I SHOULD NOT PUT ANY LIMIT ON THE LENGTH OF TIME THE RELATIONSHIP NEEDS TO MATURE AND BLOSSOM.

SIGNED THIS _____ DAY OF _____ 19___

_____

Exercises for Removing Obstacles

I. Visualization:

- Write down ten statements about your future relationships that create success images in your mind. Rules:

  a. All statements must be made in the present tense. Example: I am . . . NOT: I'll be . . .

  b. All statements must be made in the affirmative. Example: I enjoy meeting people of the opposite sex. NOT: I won't be shy anymore.
  Example: I enjoy walking hand in hand with someone I love.
  Example: People find me attractive and interesting.

II. Vacuum:

- Take a look at your calendar and circle those times that you can devote to your campaign. Include lunch hours, breakfasts prior to work, and times for coffee right after work.

- Are there any associations that hinder your ability to develop new relationships? What can you do to disentangle yourself from them?

III. Ambivalence:

- Make two lists. On one, write down all the advantages of remaining single. On the other, write all the advantages of developing a permanent relationship. Decide which list best reflects your current needs. (You can't have both.) Now, destroy the list that you discarded, and get on with your campaign. If, however, you decided that you prefer singlehood, at least for now, your search is over.

IV. Rejection:

- Reread the five ways of overcoming the fear of rejection. Write down ways you can implement these ideas in your everyday life. Ask yourself: "How would my daily behavior change if I could learn to overcome my fear of rejection?"

Chapter Four

Thrive on Your Uniqueness

———————◆———————

Imagine that you are the head of a Madison Avenue advertising agency which has just been hired to promote a product and help it reach its desired market. In order for you to present the product in the best possible way, you would probably want to answer a number of questions, such as: What's unique about the product? How does it benefit the potential customer? How can we communicate its unique features and benefits to those we're trying to reach?

Whether you realize it or not, when searching for the love of your life, you are involved in the process of marketing yourself to potential partners. After all, don't you want to be liked, to make a good impression, and, finally, to become irresistible to someone special? You have probably never thought of finding love in these terms before. In fact, the idea that you are marketing yourself may seem foreign to you —

perhaps even crass. I fully understand that. Most people refuse to see themselves in the role of "selling." Of course, these are the same people who preen in front of a mirror for two hours prior to a date, who invest $300 in a new outfit, or who wouldn't be caught dead driving anything less than a late-model car — all because of a desire to make the "right" impression.

What makes the mating game so challenging and so much fun is that while you are marketing yourself, you are also shopping. Not only are you eager to be appealing, you are also looking for a special audience: a person or persons whom you want to attract. But that's another matter.

One of the biggest mistakes most people make in marketing themselves is that they try to imitate others. Today, there are so many men and women who look, talk, and act alike that it's often hard to distinguish between these apparent clones. I suspect that the mass media has much to do with it. We are all exposed to the same role models. (I wonder how many women asked for a Princess Di hairdo after watching the royal wedding.) As a result, our society is becoming increasingly homogeneous. Men and women are afraid to allow their individuality to show through because it just might be frowned upon by their peers or by corporate management. Yet ask yourself, who is it that you tend to notice, remember, and admire? Isn't it the person who, in some small way, is delightfully different from the rest?

In this chapter, we'll explore together *your* special properties, *your* interests, and *your* preferences. The idea behind this is to help you understand fully who you are and what you can bring to a relationship. Why is this important? Because, to market yourself successfully, you must know and believe in your uniqueness.

A few years ago, a crusty old salesman told me the difference between a good marketer and a confidence man.

According to him, a good salesperson believes in what he is selling. A con man doesn't. How does this relate to you? Unless you know what your best features are, it's impossible for you to believe in yourself. And without believing in yourself, how can you expect to communicate your value to others with honesty and enthusiasm? In other words, if you don't really believe that a POS would be lucky to have you as a mate, aren't you, in effect, trying to "con" him/her?

When I talk about the notion that you are going to be "selling" yourself, I certainly don't expect you to try to directly persuade others to fall in love with you. That would be ridiculous. Rather, every action you perform, from the way you walk to the way you smile, will communicate to a POS whether you believe in yourself or not. To market yourself well, you need to fully appreciate your uniqueness. Or, as any good salesperson would say, "You've got to know the product." With this aim in mind, let's begin by studying and answering these three classic marketing questions as they apply to you:

I. What's unique about me?
II. What can I offer a suitable POS?
III. How do I communicate my uniqueness to a potential mate?

I. *What's Unique About Me?*

First, let's talk about you — the qualities that make you special. This is not an easy subject to discuss because it causes many to feel uncomfortable. Most of us have a difficult time accepting ourselves fully. We carry inside us all sorts of demons. Some people set standards of external beauty that are impossible to meet. Others strive to please long-deceased parents. It seems that most of us find little ways with which to belittle ourselves. Ask us to describe our faults, and we proceed with a lengthy litany of inadequacies. Ask us to mention our attributes, and we stammer incoherently.

Bernard Haldane, one of the pioneers in the field of career counseling, believes there are three reasons why so many have a hard time discussing their strengths: First, they are taught from childhood never to brag. The truly virtuous are supposed to take their strengths and accomplishments for granted and concentrate all their efforts on improving their weak spots. And how does one go about improving the weak spots? Why, by learning from one's mistakes, of course. The fallacy of this teaching is vividly described in this excerpt from *Alice in Wonderland*:

> Alice: Where I come from, people study what they are not good at in order to be able to do what they ARE good at.

> Mad Hatter: We only go around in circles here in Wonderland, but we always end up where we started. Would you mind explaining yourself?

> Alice: Well, grown-ups tell us to find out what we did wrong and never do it again.

> Mad Hatter: That's odd! It seems to me that in order to find out about something, you have to study it. And when you study it, you should become better at it. Why should you want to become better at something and then never do it again? But please continue.

> Alice: Nobody ever tells us to study the right things we do. We're only supposed to learn from the wrong things. But we are permitted to study the right things other people do. And sometimes we are even told to copy them.

Mad Hatter: That's cheating!

Alice: You're quite right, Mr. Hatter. I do live in a topsy-turvy world. It seems like I have to do something wrong, first, in order to learn from that what not to do. And then, by not doing what I'm not supposed to do, perhaps I'll be right. But I'd rather be right the first time, wouldn't you?

As a result of this confusion in values, most of us fail to distinguish between true modesty and false modesty. The result? Not wanting to be considered vain, we hide our strengths, even from ourselves.

What are the differences between true and false modesty? Here's an example of false modesty: A woman, who, for the past twenty years, has perfected the art of knitting, is complimented on her latest project. She replies, "This little rag? Why, it's nothing at all. My cat could have knitted this better." On the other hand, true modesty is manifested when one is fully aware of her strengths but realizes that those strengths do not make her superior to anyone else. A good reply to the compliment would have been simply, "Thank you. I do enjoy knitting." A mature person knows that her strengths are what make her what she is: unique.

If you have been indoctrinated with the "virtue" of being meek, you may, initially, have difficulty in thinking of your strengths. If this is the case, simply think of them as your personality assets. Like good business people who must know their net worth, you must also know your personal strengths. In other words, in order to know your true value, you must take full inventory of your abilities.

The second reason why most people become tongue-tied about their strengths and accomplishments is because they fail to recognize that their abilities are, indeed, special. Our society gives tremendous recognition to those who have talents which are easily demonstrable. A Lawrence Olivier, a Barbra Streisand, or a Reggie Jackson have skills that receive immediate plaudits. These people cannot help but be aware of their strengths.

But what about the majority of us who have less identifiable skills? Because we do not normally receive applause for our hidden talents, we tend to diminish their importance. The mother who has tremendous insight into her children, the supervisor who is known for being able to keep a stressful situation under control, or the loyal friend who can always be counted on often think nothing of their accomplishments and strengths. That's why, when asked about their uniqueness, they remain tongue-tied.

The third reason many are not aware of their true abilities is because they have denied them to themselves. Although there is less pressure today than in the past, many still try to become what their parents and communities uphold as the right career or behavior. Dennis, a psychologist, told me about his high school years in a small town in Texas, "You just weren't considered manly unless you played high school football. So for four years, I played a game which I grew to detest. The worst part, all through my high school and college years, I thought there was something seriously wrong with me because I didn't like football."

My friend, I have a question for you. If you don't think of yourself as special, why should anyone else? All the makeup, expensive clothes, and Piaget watches in the world cannot substitute for lack of self-acceptance. You can't "con" people for very long. Eventually, they will begin to know how you feel about yourself. It's a bit like the classic conversation between patient and psychiatrist:

Patient: Doctor, why does everyone keep stepping on me?

Doctor: Why do you choose to lie down?

Do you still fight the notion that you are special? Then please, consider this: Although there are over four billion people on this earth, there is no one quite like you. No one has your exact combination of genes, nor do they have your background. No one smiles just like you or experiences life from your perspective. You are an original, a masterpiece — yes, even if you don't think so. In addition, you have probably accomplished far more than you may have imagined. You have touched the lives of others and made an impact far beyond your expectations. You are, indeed, special!

"But, Ben," some of you are thinking, "I have really 'screwed up.'" I know. So have I. So have the people you are so eager to meet. That's part of what makes us all human. I am not naive. I realize that infusing you with this not-very-original-but-true inspirational message is certainly not going to be enough to help you recognize your many qualities. You need some concrete information — proof, if you will — of why you are special. Your growing sense of self-confidence and identity will emerge as a result of your knowing your strengths and achievements.

In order to help you understand your uniqueness, therefore, you need to change your role from observer (reader) to participant (writer). Please take the time to do the exercises that follow. They are *vital* to your success. If you are like me, a bit lazy and sometimes rebellious, you may feel like skipping over these exercises. Please, *please* don't. It is simply not possible to get the maximum out of this book without actively getting involved in every aspect of your campaign. And if you think that you can properly complete this work in a half hour or so, you are mistaken. In fact, why don't you schedule an evening or two to thoroughly go through the exercises in this and in the next chapters.

61

Your Achievements

Some of the best clues to your uniqueness can be seen in your past achievements. That's because, throughout your life, you have been demonstrating your strong qualities in all that you have done. I realize that some of you are still insisting that you have not achieved all that much. Please, bear with me. You will happily discover how wrong you are.

What is achievement? According to Haldane, an achievement must have the following characteristics:

1. You must feel that you have done something well.
2. You enjoyed doing it.
3. You were proud of your accomplishment.

Notice that with this definition of achievement, the opinions of others do not matter. In other words, if you did something that no one knows about but you believe fulfills the three criteria above, it is an achievement. Conversely, if an action or experience you were involved with elicited the approval of the entire world but meant nothing to you, it should not be considered an achievement. This is a wonderful way to think of the whole concept of achieving. It takes into account not only what you are good at but also what motivates you. Therefore, in order to qualify as an achievement, an experience must carry with it a personal feeling of excellence, joy, pride, or satisfaction.

How far into the past should you search your mind for achievements? As far back as you can remember. One of the most significant accomplishments we all experience comes from the first time we did something without the help of an adult, like our first walk without an extended hand. Of course, few of us can remember such early events. But there are others that come at age seven or eight which you may well recall, such as answering a difficult question at school, hitting your first home run, aiding an elderly person across the street, helping Dad build a shed, persuading Mom to let you keep the stray dog, or taking your very first solo bicycle ride.

Later on, as adults, your list of achievements could include such things as getting the first job, dressing well with a limited budget, helping others through volunteer activities, saving money for the company, being a wonderful cook, growing a vegetable garden, helping a former spouse get through medical school, losing twenty pounds, earning a degree, being elected to a local or national board, fixing the old Rambler, running your first marathon, or raising fine children without the help of a spouse. The list is endless. Life is full of accomplishments, both big and small, and each of us can lay claim to our share.

Now that you have an idea of what is meant by achievements, you can probably think of many. Write down a list of no fewer than twenty. When you do, make sure the list covers every aspect of your life, from childhood on. Include school, family life, social activities, community activities, your career, and personal relationships. Be as specific as possible. For each one, answer the following four questions:

1. What was the achievement?
2. How was it accomplished?
3. What were the results?
4. What made it important to you?

Having compiled a list of at least twenty of your achievements, circle the ten that are most significant to you. Now, imagine for a moment that you are Sherlock Holmes, and begin searching for clues from your list. For example, what do you consider your number one achievement, your number two achievement, and so on? What do you think they say about the kind of person you are? Are your achievements people-oriented, career-oriented, project-oriented, or sports-oriented? These are valuable clues. Do they give you any hints as to what type of individual you would be comfortable with? Are your achievements related to each other? If so, in what way?

Writing this list will enlighten you and make you aware of your many accomplishments. As a result, your self-esteem will be elevated. Over and over again, I have seen people who had previously suffered from a lack of self-worth begin to see themselves in a new light after compiling this type of list. Why? Because they now see a lifetime of accomplishments written down in black and white. They can no longer ignore them.

Your Inventory of Strengths

In addition to unearthing your past achievements, you need to take time to discover your present strengths. We all have talents and interests that are unique only to us, but they tend to get buried in the general rush of everyday life. Often, people take their strengths for granted. Many believe that, if they possess a particular skill or have a special interest, everyone else in the world does, too. For instance, the amateur athlete feels that anyone can hit a home run, the businessperson doesn't think there's anything special about knowing how to price a product, and the fabulous cook thinks little of his/her culinary ability. But that's faulty thinking. Each one of us has a unique combination of talents and interests. As a wise man told me a few years ago, "We are all geniuses in some things and retarded in others."

The following is an inventory list of strengths and interests encompassing the full range of human activity. This list is inspired by work conducted by Dr. Lila Swell as described in her book, *Success, You Can Make It Happen* (see Bibliography). Next to each strength you feel applies to you, write down one example of how you have recently seen it being manifested in your life.

Strength:	Evidence:
I am sensitive to others.	Ex: John, my older boy, was in a bad mood. I was able to help him open up and discuss his problem with me.
I am articulate.	Ex: At the last department meeting, I was able to explain the reasons why we need to exchange our type-writers for word processors. My boss complimented me on my report.

Strength: **Evidence:**

Personality:

I am:

- flexible
- persuasive
- natural
- honest
- courageous
- direct
- fair
- determined
- able to enjoy humor
- dynamic
- stimulating
- enthusiastic
- charming
- assertive

Strength: **Evidence**

- elegant
- fun-loving
- responsible
- confident
- out-going
- dedicated
- vivacious
- introspective
- gentle
- passionate
- neat
- charismatic
- open

Emotions:

I am:

- able to show my feelings
- generous toward others
- warm toward others
- sensitive to others' needs
- able to empathize
- responsive to others
- kind
- able to inspire confidence in others
- considerate
- compassionate
- thoughtful
- forgiving
- loving

Intelligence:

I am:

- a good listener

Strength: **Evidence:**

- intuitive
- a good speaker
- able to reason well
- analytical
- perceptive
- bright
- wise
- a deep thinker
- logical
- witty
- insightful
- able to remember well
- intellectually curious
- a good writer
- quick-minded
- able to grasp concepts
- articulate

Aesthetics:

I am:

- good at using color
- artistically creative
- resourceful
- inventive
- spontaneous
- imaginative
- able to coordinate furnishings
- able to arrange food and flowers
- good at gardening
- able to play a musical instrument
- able to coordinate fashion
- able to appreciate good art

Strength: **Evidence:**

- able to appreciate music
- able to sing
- able to act
- able to paint or draw
- able to dance
- able to design
- able to work with crafts

Practical/Mechanical Abilities:
I am:

- able to fix things around the house
- a good cook
- able to repair engines
- a good carpenter
- a good seamstress
- good at knitting
- a good host/hostess
- good at budgeting
- good at investing money
- a good parent

Physical Appearance/Athletics:
I am:

- energetic
- filled with stamina
- coordinated
- agile
- fast
- competitive
- well-proportioned
- in good physical shape
- attractive

Strength: **Evidence:**

Sexuality:

I am:
- an experienced lover
- a sensitive lover
- a versatile lover
- a responsive lover
- a good cuddler
- physically demonstrative

Take a look at all your strengths. If anything, you should develop a deep respect for the kind of person you are. It's as if you are looking at a different kind of mirror, one that does not lie. I hope that you are impressed with yourself. Now, you need to analyze this new portrait. What kind of pattern or patterns do you see? For example, are you physically-oriented? Or are you, perhaps, an intellectual with strong emotional strengths? Whoever you are, whatever your greatest interests are, you should be able to acquire valuable knowledge from a close examination of the task you just completed. And this knowledge, in addition to giving you confidence in your "marketability" to a POS, should also give you more information as to the type of life and, therefore, the kind of mate who will suit you best.

The Sales Presentation

Let us return to the marketing analogy. Now that you have defined your many individual strengths and enumerated your achievements, it's time to put all these factors into a cohesive presentation. You are now ready to answer the question: "What makes me unique?"

Write a one- or two-page description of yourself as exemplified by your greatest strengths and achievements. Discuss your strong points with some evidence to illustrate them. Brag a little! While remaining completely truthful, you should write this presentation in the most positive light possible. So if anyone says to you, "Tell me about yourself," you can present your best qualities in such a concise and clear way that there will be no question what it is that makes you special. To get the most from this exercise, avoid making general statements without offering specific examples. The more specific you are, the clearer will emerge the picture of your personality. Here's an example of a written self-portrait developed by a friend of mine:

> My life revolves around my career, my family, my friends, and sports. I consider my first achievement to be the fact that I was the very first girl to be selected to play on my class softball team. That was after I hit three home runs as a last-minute substitute. In high school, I joined the track team and broke the school's broad jump record for women. This and other early experiences taught me that I am a goal-oriented person who is dedicated to succeeding. I still spend an hour five times a week exercising and staying in shape.

> Although I didn't actively seek this, I've developed a large number of friends over the years. I am a good friend because I accept others and try never to judge actions. I'm also a really good listener. Recently, a friend told me some very intimate things, and I was able to offer my support and empathy. This made me feel good.

> Excelling in my career is also important to me. In the past four years, I have received five promotions. One of

70

these promotions was as a result of my inventing a new management technique that improved productivity by 20%.

I have strong intellectual curiosity, particularly about national events. I especially enjoy discussing politics with others, even if we happen to disagree.

I consider my greatest achievement to be the raising of my two children. In spite of my career, I've made time to be a sensitive, nurturing parent. I also have a wonderful friendship with my children.

To summarize, one could say that I am an athletic, career-minded individual who is a good friend, enjoys parenthood, and likes to discuss national politics in her spare time. Oh yes, although you wouldn't mistake me for a Hollywood starlet, I make up in personality, vitality, and sexual energy what I lack in looks and figure.

Now I don't know about you, but that's what I'd call an engaging portrait of a high-achieving woman. In fact, aren't you curious about meeting her? This same woman, before doing the exercises, resisted the notion that there was anything special about her. Now, armed with the knowledge of her uniqueness, she presents a clearly defined picture of her most important strengths and accomplishments. Notice how she handled a potential drawback (her less-than-perfect physical appearance) in an extremely positive, up-beat manner.

You will also realize your "specialness" by completing the exercises in this chapter and writing your own self-portrait. (I know that among you there are a few die-hards who are still trying to benefit from this book without doing any of the work. Sorry, but without some pain, no gain. So go back three steps, do not collect $200, and start doing the exercises.)

Once you write your self-portrait, make a point of reading it to yourself on a daily basis. This will help remind you that you are not dealing with just anyone, but with *someone* quite special who deserves to find loving companionship.

II. What Can I Offer a Suitable POS?

Rick is a handsome, well-groomed, and intelligent twenty-four-year-old single. He is also frustrated. "I really want to get married," he told me, "but I can't seem to find anyone suitable." "Why is that?" I asked incredulously, knowing quite a few young women who would enjoy getting to know Rick. But after listening to him, his problem made a lot of sense. "It's hard to find genuine people," he confided. "For instance, when I go out with someone to a movie, I like to ask her afterwards what she thought of it. In almost every situation I can recall, my dates answered me by first asking me what I thought. It's as if they're afraid to tell me how they really feel for fear that I won't agree with them. Or, if a girl does tell me she liked the movie, and I tell her that I didn't, she'll often back down with something like, 'Yeah, I guess you're right.' This drives me crazy. It seems that so many of the girls I date are so concerned with becoming what they think I want them to be that I never get to know who they really are. I don't know why it's so hard for them to just tell me their feelings. It's almost like a ball of mush in front of you saying, 'Tell me what you want me to be and I'll be it.' Of course, in the long run, this never works. No one can hide forever from being herself. So people get married, never knowing who they're married to until it's too late . . . Why can't I find a girl who will not be afraid to be herself from the very beginning? It would be so refreshing."

Ultimately, what each of us has to offer the world is ourselves. We can never be more than second-rate imitations of something we are not, but we can always be "originals" as ourselves.

Unfortunately, many men and women have not accepted themselves fully. One reason is that, during childhood, they did not experience the joys of unconditional love. Unconditional love states: "I love you the same way all the time, no matter what." Conditional, or neurotic, love states: "If you behave the way I want you to, I will love you."

For those of us who have never experienced the warmth and security of unconditional love (this includes most people, since parents are rarely more self-actualized than their offspring), it is difficult to show our authenticity. Instead of confidently manifesting "the real us" — warts and all — we keep seeking approval from others. We silently wonder, "If you really knew me, would you still love me?" Therefore, during the process of developing new relationships, we tend to seek the approval of POS by behaving the way we think they want us to behave rather than by simply being ourselves. As a result, our companions cannot get to know who we are. As Rick spoke of his last girlfriend, "When I talked to her, I never really knew what she wanted or how she felt because she always tried to second-guess me. I can't be attracted to someone who doesn't have an identity — a core. Frankly, it's a turn-off."

You, my friend, have just gone through a series of exercises designed to help you develop a clear grasp of who you are. You have written a self-portrait that lists your most attractive characteristics. If you did the exercises thoroughly, you should be quite impressed with your uniqueness. Be proud of that. Accept yourself. And yes, learn to love who you are.

The Bible invokes: "Love thy neighbor *as* thyself." Notice that it doesn't say, "Love thy neighbor more than thyself." That's because it's impossible for a person to like or love anyone else more than they like or love themselves. What we project to others is a mirror of our own feelings. A person who is intolerant of others is, most likely, intolerant of himself; a person who has difficulty showing affection probably doesn't treat himself kindly, either. The more accepting you are of *you*, the more likely you'll accept others. The more you learn to love yourself, the more you will be able to offer love to someone special. Ultimately, the greatest gift you can offer a loved one is your unabashed, self-accepting, self-loving you.

When I talk about self-love, I do not mean the narcissistic kind of self-absorption that excludes everyone else. On the contrary, men and women who accept themselves, who love themselves, who are at peace with themselves, are much more able to focus on the interests and needs of others. It is the person with insecurities who must constantly feed the famished ego and, in the process, becomes self-absorbed.

Accepting Others

Aside from showing you how unique you are, listing your strengths and achievements has a hidden benefit: It should help you accept the fact that everyone is special in his/her own way. Something quite wonderful happens when we accept the individuality of *all* human beings. It allows us to feel special, not at the expense of others, but by sharing our own humanity with them. We begin to realize that the term "special" does not mean "better." Instead, it means distinctive, unique, individuated.

This is an important topic to bring up for the following reason: There are some who have extreme difficulty in forming relationships with POS because they have developed a destructive attitude toward others. Unlike the all-embracing, people-loving attitude that acknowledges the uniqueness of all human beings, their attitude is judgmental and elitist.

Kathy is an extremely attractive woman of thirty-six. She has never married, yet she is forever searching for her special man. In contrast, her single girlfriends, most of whom are considerably less attractive, have reasonably active social lives. Kathy, on the other hand, consistently chides them for their low standards. "I wouldn't go out with someone unless the magic was there," she often says. Even when she dates, Kathy remains critical and aloof. She is so successful in making men feel inadequate that most of her relationships (the few she does have) are short-lived.

Why would anyone sabotage his/her chances at love by deliberately discouraging relationships with POS? There are several reasons:

1. Fear of rejection. If we set standards that are impossible to meet, we end up rejecting, thus avoiding the possibility of being rejected by others.

2. Fear of intimacy. Those who set impossibly high standards can back out of a relationship before it becomes too intimate. This way, they never have to confront their fear of making a commitment by exposing their inner selves to someone else.

3. Parental fixation. Some men and women so idealize the kind of marriage and devotion they witnessed in their parents' home that they become obsessed with trying to duplicate that kind of relationship.

Of course, a child's vision of his parents is often distorted, making the attempt at duplicating the fantasy even more difficult, if not impossible.

Still others have a fixation on a parent, usually of the opposite sex. They compare POS to their Super Dad or Super Mom. No one can withstand the competition with childhood deities.

4. A distorted self-concept. Some children are raised with the belief they are so special that nothing is quite good enough for them. Being brought up in a self-indulgent, overprotective environment leads them to think that others exist solely to take care of their needs. For these "princes" and "princesses," the adjustment to a world of give-and-take is particularly painful.

Do you suffer from the feeling that you are more special than most people? If so, you may be creating a self-destructive shield that is protecting you from developing a caring relationship with another human being. As I just explained (this is worth repeating), the exercises you just completed in this chapter should help you understand that everyone has his/her achievements and unique qualities — that everyone is special in one way or another — that everyone has some things that are unmistakably original about him/her.

This realization should enable you to now look at others in a fresh, new way. Instead of focusing on what they lack (after all, are you so perfect that you can afford to judge others?), you can learn to appreciate them for their particular set of strengths and abilities.

So, in asking the second marketing question, "What do I have to offer others?", the answer is twofold:

1. Your unabashed, self-accepting, self-loving, unique-in-all-the-world self.

2. The respect you can give others in recognition of the fact that they, too, are a one-of-a-kind phenomenon, just like you.

Dealing with the Warts

I know what some of you are thinking. It might be something like, "All this is fine and good, Ben, but you don't understand my problem. I'm thirty pounds overweight" (or "I don't have enough education," or "I'm too old," or "Women just don't find me attractive," and so on). Do you feel defeated before you've even started? Are you of the opinion that this book is written for everyone else but you?

Let me give you some good news:

1. Natural beauty is no guarantee of marital happiness. Linda Evans, Elizabeth Taylor, Tom Selleck, and Burt Reynolds are just some of the many "beautiful people" for whom marital bliss had been elusive. On the other hand, there are many men and women who do not look like the latest starved-thin starlet or a muscle-bound Schwartzenegger who have wonderful marriages.

    Pat, a dear friend of mine, exemplifies the kind of person who does not let physical imperfections control her life. Pat is not just thirty pounds overweight; she's considerably heavier than that.

77

But she doesn't let that stand in her way. She is a vibrant, self-assured lady who is one of the most loved women I know. And although she is happily married, Pat, because she likes who she is, creates the kind of sexual vibrancy that makes men attracted to her.

Don't let a temporary, or even permanent, arrangement of skin, bones, and lymphatic tissue make you defensive about your appearance. It may sound trite, but real beauty comes from the inner glow of those who love themselves and who love others. This doesn't mean that you don't have a responsibility to look your best. You do. The secret is to look *your* best, not Mel Gibson's or Sharon Stone's.

2 You don't have to be *like* anyone else. Did you know there are at least sixteen different personality types? Some people are extroverted, some are introverted. Some are practical, others are visionary. Some have high energy, others are more "laid back." No one person can appeal to everyone. And, like Rick's girlfriends, those who spend all their efforts trying to be liked by others can appear to be lacking in individuality. Of course, exercising common courtesy is important, as is having a basic understanding of people skills, but the neurotic need to agree with everyone goes far beyond what Dale Carnegie had in mind.

3 People who are not self-conscious are attractive regardless of their handicaps. Itzhak Perlman is so matter-of-fact about his polio-stricken legs that he has been able to overcome audiences' discomfort

with and prejudice toward performers in wheel chairs. Ray Charles, Jose Feliciano, and Stevie Wonder have achieved fame and fortune in spite of their blindness. And, in a much lighter vein, comedienne Joan Rivers has transformed her flat chest into a treasure chest by making fun of her underdeveloped mammaries.

Why did these wonderful people succeed? For the same reason you can: They concentrated on their strengths while accepting their weaknesses. They have turned their stumbling blocks into stepping stones.

Do you have imperfections? So do I. So does everyone. But remember, *you* are special because of your many strengths, not your weak spots. So get over your hang-ups and get on with it. The world is filled with other wonderfully imperfect people who are eager to meet you. (More on this in chapter five.)

III. How Do I Communicate My Uniqueness?

In advertising, creating a clearly defined image in the minds of people is called "positioning." Our brains are cluttered with so much information that we like to identify products by one attribute. Coke is the "real thing," Avis tries harder, and Northwestern is the "quiet company."

The same is true of personalities. Think for a moment. Which actor was better known, Clark Gable or Van Heflin? Clark Gable, of course. Yet many believe that Van Heflin was a much better actor. Why, then, was Gable so much more celebrated? The answer is positioning. Van Heflin always "became" the character he played until little of his personality remained. Gable, on the other hand, was always Gable. He became easily identifiable in the minds of his audiences. Frankly, my dear, you couldn't miss his style, even if you didn't give a damn.

How can you use positioning in your search for permanent love? There are hundreds of ways. People are attracted to others who have something unique about them. In turn, if you use your uniqueness or specialty as a barrier-breaker, you will always have something fascinating to talk about. Look at your inventory of strengths to see which would be socially beneficial attributes. For example, do you play a musical instrument? Are you an expert on anything, from collecting butterflies to World War II airplanes? Do you dress in a distinctive manner, speak a foreign language, tell funny jokes at a party, sport a handlebar moustache, or sketch people? Have you lived on a farm and raised animals? Any skill or trait that makes you distinctive can be an excellent way for you to position yourself clearly in the minds of POS. By the sheer fact that you stand out from the crowd, you will appeal to some people. In addition, you will immediately be placed on common ground with those who have similar interests.

Do you feel there is nothing special that you know or care about? Then perhaps apathy is part of your problem. Don't be like the man on the street who was asked what he thought of ignorance and apathy. "I don't know, and I don't care," was his laconic reply. Find something to care about, whether it's a hobby or a volunteer job. You will discover that your new enthusiasm will make you more vibrant and, therefore, more attractive. There's nothing more appealing than a person who cares deeply about something.

In a way, it takes courage to position oneself clearly. While it is true that some people will find you immediately attractive, others will not identify with you at all. On the whole, I consider this a positive. After all, you are not running a campaign to be Mr. or Ms. Popularity. Instead, you are going through a selection process to find potentially suitable mates. Just like the Marines, you are looking for a few good (wo)men. Look, even Tide, the top-selling detergent, is liked by fewer than thirty percent of the detergent buyers. That's like being rejected by seven out of ten consumers. But the producers of Tide, through positioning, have developed a secure niche in the minds of customers. And you can do the same when it comes to you and POS.

Take a close look at what you have accomplished! In this chapter, you've started to uncover the real you. If you've ever doubted it before, you should now know that you are a special, lovable person who has much to offer another. Now, let's turn our attention to your future mate. Who is that special person? What must he or she possess in order to be compatible with and attractive to you? In the next chapter, this is precisely what you'll find out.

Chapter Five

What Color Is Your Paradise?

A few months ago, while driving, I passed by a busy intersection where I saw a sight eerily reminiscent of the 1930s. A young man stood at the corner carrying an oversized sign which commanded bluntly: "HIRE ME! YOU WON'T BE SORRY." What happened to the young man remains a mystery; I don't know if he got hired or not. Nevertheless, I am quite sure of one thing. If, indeed, he did land a job from that experience, it would have been a dead-end, no-chance-for-advancement type of position. This young man was selling himself short. Why? Instead of focusing his efforts on finding a *fulfilling* occupation, he was attempting to satisfy only his short-term needs.

Are you carrying a big sign saying: "LOVE ME! YOU WON'T BE SORRY."? If you are unclear about the kind of person that would be compatible with you, you might as well be. In the previous chapter, you learned how unique you are. Doesn't it make sense, then, that you should have certain preferences when seeking the love of your life?

Discovering what is really important to you, however, is not so simple. The process of learning what you want in a mate can be confounding. Why? Because of the influences of outside forces. Here's an example: Amanda is a twenty-eight-year-old school teacher. She is determined to marry a doctor. Her mother, a domineering woman, planted and then nurtured this thought in Amanda's mind throughout her childhood. In spite of the fact that she has been attracted to a number of her male colleagues, Amanda has consistently avoided becoming seriously involved with any of them simply because they didn't have "M.D." in back of their names.

Shortly after meeting Amanda, I saw a vivid though fictional illustration of this stubborn insistence on choosing the profession rather than the person. This happened while watching a rerun of the popular TV sitcom, "Barney Miller." Sergeant Harris, the handsome black detective who is forever yearning for "the good life" and who probably spends a better part of his paycheck on expensive sports coats (he always looks good), is sitting at his desk at headquarters when in walks a gorgeous woman. She is a nurse from the health department who has come to the police station to inoculate the men against a possible epidemic of smallpox Upon seeing this lovely vision, Harris jumps to his feet and begins exercising his well-practiced charm. After several unsuccessful attempts at engaging her in conversation, he realizes that his easy chitchat is not producing the desired effect; she remains cold and aloof. Finally, in total frustration, he asks if she is either married or engaged, to which she replies, "Not yet, but I will be soon." "What does that mean? What's his name?" asks the now-intimidated and confused Sergeant Harris. "I don't know his name, yet. But I guarantee it will be something like Dr. Cohen or Dr. Sheppard or Dr. Eastman." Poor Sergeant Harris didn't stand a chance; after all, he was just a cop.

In addition to parental and self-imposed conditioning, there are other aspects that can color one's search for a compatible mate. Many young men experience feelings of awakening sexuality upon sneaking their first look at the centerfold of a "girlie" magazine. This unreal "encounter" often becomes the ideal of womanhood — body make-up, filtered lenses, and all. Tragically, for many this puerile notion remains a fixed idea even into adulthood. As a result, many men chase the "approved packaging" without examining the "contents" — a poor formula for a fulfilling relationship.

And yet, on the other hand, each of us has *genuine* preferences and needs. These needs are not based on forced prejudices or teenage fantasies. Instead, they are wedded to our very own, deeply ingrained personality traits. If we ignore them, we may end up in a dead-end relationship, frustrated and unhappy. How do we uncover the "wheat" of real needs and preferences from the "chaff" of unrealistic daydreams or the imposed standards of others? The answer lies within you. Because your attraction to others is often rooted in your early life experiences, clues to the characteristics you admire most are strewn throughout your past.

Once again, I'm going to ask you to roll up your sleeves and get involved in the process of self-discovery. There is simply no way to gain insight without going through this process. And insight is what you need to aid you in your search for the love of your life.

Attractions and Detriments

Make two identical lists of no fewer than ten of the most significant POS in your past. (By significant, I mean those who have had the greatest impact on you, whether positive or negative.) Make sure that you leave enough space after each name. Next to each one, write down three positive traits that are appealing to you about that person. In each case, make sure you give one piece of evidence to illustrate this trait. If you need help in thinking about positive attributes, refer to the list in chapter four.

Once you have finished this, take the second identical list and write by each person's name the three most unappealing traits. Again, to make this meaningful, give one example of how this particular characteristic affected you personally.

In writing these adjectives, include every facet that is important to you. If physical attributes such as height and weight are significant, include them. If loud behavior repels you, mention that.

Who should be on this list? Definitely include a parent and all former spouses and other POS with whom you have had any important romantic relationships. In addition, add siblings, a grandparent, teachers or school friends, bosses, co-workers, and any other POS who may have had an influence on your life. You see, your past relationships with others of the opposite sex have contributed greatly to your present concept of what is desirable and undesirable in a POS. By doing this exercise, you will discover revealing information about what is important to you. Take as much time as you need to complete this process thoroughly. It's well worth the effort.

Next, take a pen or pencil and circle all the characteristics you included on both lists. On one sheet of paper list all the positive traits, and on another list all the negative ones. Next to each trait write down the number of times it appeared on your list. Now, rewrite both positive and negative lists, putting the most frequently repeated adjectives first, the second most repeated adjectives next, and so on.

Something very special should come out of this time-consuming but essential work. You will see clearly which personal characteristics in others attract you and which repel you. Particularly revealing is the frequency with which certain traits will surface on both sides of the ledger. One woman discovered that she was drawn to assertive men, even though she was somewhat introverted. And a teacher who was formerly married to someone incompatible discovered that physically active women attract him, a fact that fits with his own active lifestyle.

As you examine what you wrote, look out for patterns. For example, do well-organized, punctual, well-dressed people appeal to you? If all these adjectives are present, they form a clear pattern of what's important to you. If you also dislike sloppy work or slovenly appearance, the pattern is further reinforced.

What you include on your list of attributes and detriments should be quite revealing. But just as revealing are those traits you *failed* to include. Take a close look at the list you wrote and compare it to the list of personality traits in chapter four. What traits did you ignore? For example, is mechanical ability or a quick mind included on your list? If not, it could be that these are not major considerations for you. Did you include physical appearance? If you didn't, you may not need an Adonis or a Venus to satisfy your need for love.

Destructive patterns can also become visible through this exercise. Glen, an attorney in his mid-thirties, discovered that the significant women in his life have been domineering. He realized, then, that he was always attracted to women who tried to control him. He also learned that those relationships had never worked for him. As a result of this realization, he decided to go into therapy to consciously modify this destructive pattern in his life.

It's not easy to look at ourselves objectively. If, after completing this exercise, you find it difficult to interpret your emerging portrait, ask a trusted friend to help you. He or she might see some patterns that you have missed which could shed more light on what's important to you.

To complete this process and to get the most out of what you've learned, answer, in writing, the following questions:

1. What do you consider to be the non-negotiable characteristics or behavioral patterns a POS must possess in order to be a candidate for a long-term relationship with you?

2. What are the characteristics or behavioral patterns that immediately rule out a candidate for a relationship with you?

3. What characteristics seem to be unimportant to you?

4. Which flaws can you live with?

5. Which attributes can you do without?

To borrow the language of an earlier decade, these are "heavy" questions. So don't zip through them like a fakir walking on hot coals. Take your time. Think. And write down the answers as truthfully as you can.

If, I repeat, *if* you have done these and the previous exercises, you are in the unique position of being one of the few people seeking a long-term relationship who knows what to look for. You can now start funneling your efforts because you can discern more clearly who is "in the ballpark" and who is not. In addition, if these exercises revealed to you patterns and preferences that, until now, have remained submerged somewhere in your subconscious, you can take advantage of this new awareness to aid you in your search.

How Does Long-Lasting Love Happen?

Arnold, a telephone executive in the San Francisco Bay Area, was telling me how he fell in love with Penny, his wife of twenty-five years. "By the time I met Penny, I was twenty-seven. To be perfectly honest, I was eager to get married. I had dated a great deal and, yes, I proposed to several women, each of whom turned me down. In each situation prior to meeting Penny, I always felt that I had to work hard to keep the relationship going. But the moment I met her, we both felt different. It was as if we'd known each other all our lives. We felt completely natural."

Most people talk about "being in love" as if it were a clearly defined concept that is understood by everyone. You and I have managed to discuss the subject for quite a while now without even defining what is meant when we speak of love. And yet, in talking with many, there was a general disagreement as to what love really is. An astounding number of men and women told me, in private, that they were not quite sure if they had ever *really* been in love. This presents a definite challenge. How can men and women find the love of their life if they don't even know the nature of romantic love?

The process of falling in love has always been shrouded in mystery. There are numerous theories on the subject, as contradictory as "opposites attract" to "all couples begin to look alike." What is the truth, anyway? What are the ingredients that make for long-lasting love? How do you even know if you are involved in a genuine love relationship?

The Shock of Recognition

In his book, *The Psychology of Romantic Love*, (see Bibliography) Nathaniel Branden describes what happens when people discover the potential for love in each other:

> Still, in the early stages of a new relationship, and sometimes even in the first moment of meeting, it is not uncommon for future lovers to experience a sudden "shock of recognition," an odd sense of familiarity, a sense of encountering a person already known on some level and in some mysterious, seemingly inexplicable way.

This is exactly what happened to Arnold and Penny when they met. They "recognized" each other even though they were strangers. In their case, they shared a deep faith in the same religion and a clear priority of centering their lives around children and family. And yet, they are hardly carbon copies. Each of them has distinctly different traits that the other finds fascinating.

Consider another couple, Nancy and Ben (my wife and me). On the surface, our backgrounds could not be more dissimilar. I was born in Tel Aviv, Israel, and Nancy was raised in a small farming community in southern Ohio. And yet, when we first met, we immediately felt at ease with each other. At the same time, we were terribly fascinated by our differences. How was it possible that the two of us were able to share the same view on life? I don't know, but we found ourselves interested in the same things. More importantly, we saw the world in much the same way. For example, we are both intuitive about people and enjoy understanding them beyond the surface. We also share a deep love for the arts and travel. But the most significant aspect of our relationship, by far, is our mutual need to be independent of other people's control over our lives. As a result, we chose, during the first year of our marriage, to take a chance on self-employment at the risk of giving up the security of jobs.

The Germans have a word, "Weltanschauung," which roughly translates to "a view of the world, the way a person views life." Each of us has deeply held beliefs and convictions about the world, ourselves, and life as a whole. We may see our life as a constant adventure, or we can see it as a pre-ordained tragedy. We may view our role as passive observer or as conqueror. We may feel that the world is filled with beauty and life or with ugliness and treachery. We may see ourselves as children of God or as part of a meaningless cosmic joke. Whether we are exuberant or pessimistic, defiant or resigned, is determined by our Weltanschauung.

This view of life is the framework from which we perceive the world and through which we interpret events in our lives. Whether we take risks or take steps to minimize them, whether we are predominantly joyful or fearful, is all part of our Weltanschauung. When two people meet who share the same sense of what life means to them, they "recognize" each other. It's like twins who meet after having been unaware of each other's existence. "Finally, somebody truly understands me," they might say to themselves, feeling a new sense of validation. "At last, there is someone else, a soul mate who perceives life as I do." It is a wonderful feeling of bonding, based on shared perceptions and priorities.

In earlier times, it was relatively easy to find a person with

91

the same view of life. Communities tended to be inbred, where all the members of a particular church or synagogue were inclined to marry each other. Under those specific conditions, finding someone who shared the same outlook on life was not at all out of the ordinary. Today, however, especially in large urban areas, people lead isolated lives away from their familiar neighborhoods and cultural heritage. The "shock of recognition" then becomes more acute and, therefore, more crucial.

But similarities aren't enough. Most of us would be terribly bored with someone who is our mirror image. Once we find an individual who shares our sense of life, the differences between us become complementary rather than separative. John, a successful corporate owner with no artistic interests, is fascinated by his wife's profession as a modern dance teacher. Suzanne's artistic qualities are a constant source of delight to him, just as his boundless energy and drive are a source of awe and respect for her. Although they have major differences, they share a strong commitment to family and the work ethic, based on their midwestern Protestant upbringing.

Margaret, a successful advertising executive, is engaged to Joseph, a droll professor of medieval history who loves to garden. He derives energy from her enthusiasm, and she is able to "wind down" with her botanically-minded mate. In spite of their differences, Margaret and Joseph, both orphaned as children, have developed the kind of intimacy that allows them to talk about their feelings freely — something fundamental to their happiness which neither was able to do in any previous relationship.

In each of these situations, the foundation of sharing the same view of life is the basis for agreement. Beyond that, each person enjoys the fascinating differences of the other.

How does all this apply to you? In order to know the

"color of your paradise," you need to know what you're looking for. Sometimes, lonely people who are eager to develop a love relationship try to make the proverbial round peg fit into the square hole, making an attempt to seek agreement where none exists. If you have to *work* at finding agreement — if each time you meet with a particular POS you feel that you have to "work hard" or to "prove yourself" or act contrary to your true nature — ask yourself this: "Would I want to behave this way for the rest of my life?" Without the ability to develop genuine caring and understanding, your relationship will be that of intimate strangers.

Ask yourself another question: "What are some of the fundamental parts of my being?" If your life revolves around your religious beliefs, it may be wise to focus your dating on those whose beliefs are similar to yours. If you are an entrepreneur, just starting out, you may be wise to find a mate who is willing to share with you the risks involved and who is excited about your efforts. Or, if raising a family is the focus of your life, make sure your potential spouse shares your love for children.

Love and Self-Esteem

Another way to test the health and long-lasting potential of any relationship is to ask yourself this: "When I am with him/her, do I feel better or worse about myself?" Ultimately, your healthy self-esteem is the key to your happiness and emotional balance. No person who diminishes your sense of well-being is worth the trouble. Even if you are enjoying the most incredible sexual experience with someone, if your self-respect is torn to shreds, you are jeopardizing your emotional health and happiness. I have seen my parents tear at each other for over twenty years. Today, they are both much happier leading separate lives. So avoid destructive relationships like the plague. Find a POS who appreciates you for those qualities that you are most proud of and who encourages you to be the best you can be. When you find someone like this and then offer him/her the same understanding and encouragement, you have the basis for an ever-growing, mutually nurturing relationship.

The Age Factor

Most people have a specific age group in mind when visualizing their ideal mate. Men usually think of someone a few years younger, and women expect their men to be a bit older. This arrangement is so inbred that, until recently, it has been taken for granted. As in most cases, attitudes grow out of the needs of society. And for many years, there were convincing reasons as to why the older-man/younger-woman relationship was the rule. Until recently, the husband had the responsibility for the financial well-being of the family while the wife stayed home to take care of the children. An older man was more likely to be financially established, while the younger wife was at her primary childbearing age. The husband, then, provided security and, in return, enjoyed having a nubile bride.

But today, unless the age factor is an essential part of what's important to you in a POS, there are convincing arguments for singles to expand their search for a mate beyond the traditionally narrow chronological confines. Here are some of them:

1. Changing economic factors. Today, as society is gradually reaching job equality between men and women, the economic realities of marriage are changing. Most likely, both members of a couple

are working, with the woman often earning as much or more than her mate. Women are less likely to seek financial security in a marriage. Instead, they are more likely to look for emotional support and understanding. Indeed, because the younger generation is more comfortable with the new equality between the sexes, many older women find younger men more attractive. Conversely, many young men find the wisdom and sophistication (not to mention the financial resources) of more established women quite appealing.

2. Changing family priorities. Many of today's singles have been previously married. Having already raised children, they are no longer interested in starting new families. Therefore, their need for emotional and sexual sustenance is the primary motive for seeking a relationship. Under those circumstances, because the biological clock poses no threat, the age of either mate becomes much less of a factor.

3. "Where the boys are." While the statistics scream that there is an overabundance of women in relation to men, there are more men than women in the twenty-to-thirty age group. It only makes sense, then, that women over thirty and men under thirty would begin to become romantically involved with each other.

4. Sexuality. Men and women reach their sexual peak at different stages of their lives. For men, the time of maximum sexual drive is in their teens. But women do not reach their peak of sexuality until

95

their mid-thirties or even mid-forties. From an objective point of view, there is a strong argument for greater sexual compatibility between older women and younger men.

5.   Longevity. The U.S. census points out that women live, on the average, eight years longer than men. Today, there are millions of women who face loneliness at a time when companionship is most critical. Perhaps, if women married younger men, there might not be so many lonely widows in this world.

Am I advocating that men marry older women? Not necessarily. I simply want to illustrate that there are logical reasons to consider this kind of relationship. In fact, among sophisticated people, this type of arrangement has flourished through the ages. Samuel Johnson was devoted to a wife many years his senior. Sara Bernhardt was sixty-six when she began her affair with the thirty-one-year-old Lou Tellegen. When he wrote his autobiography, he described their relationship as "the most glorious four years of my life."

Nor should younger women necessarily avoid permanent bonding with older men. Cary, a good friend of mine, is an extremely youthful sixty-year-old psychiatrist who is deliriously happy and compatible with his twenty-four-year-old wife. They met when he, a lonely widower for eight years, was eating dinner at a restaurant where she was working part time while going to college. Because of the vast difference in age, this courageous couple had to withstand a tremendous amount of criticism and rejection from both sides of the family. (His children were particularly resentful.) But instead of deterring them, this conflict drew them together and tied them even closer. Today, they are among the happiest couples I know. In fact, they just had their first child.

In urging you to re-examine the age factor, I simply want to open a door to you that you may not have considered opening. You need to eliminate all possible obstacles to your happiness. If, however, the age of a POS is important to you and is not just a matter of blindly following conventions, then by all means, follow your sense of priorities.

The "Rich and Sexy" Trap

Rhonda, a forty-four-year-old public relations executive, was telling me what she seeks in a man. "I want him to be successful enough at what he does to make at least as much as I make." I was so curious to hear more that I ventured forth a bit hesitantly, "Would you mind telling me how much you make?" "Last year, my income was $45,000," responded Rhonda, as she straightened her back with obvious pride. "In that case, you have just eliminated well over ninety percent of the men in this country," was my blunt reply. Rhonda was shocked. "I never thought about it that way before," she said slowly. "But tell me," I persisted, "with your fine income, why do you care how much your lover or future husband makes?" Rhonda thought about this for a moment. She finally responded truthfully that she felt her friends and relatives would expect her to bring home a "prize."

This kind of thinking, that a man must make more money than a woman, is still incredibly ingrained. In spite of the fact that many women are no longer dependent financially, they still limit their search to those who earn more than they do. They want to "marry up." Are you imbued with this kind of thinking? If so, you may pass by the most eligible and, potentially, most compatible mates. Ask yourself this: "Am I looking for someone who will impress my friends and support me, or do I primarily seek emotional sustenance from my relationship?" Whatever your answer, act accordingly.

Men, too, are often stuck in a limiting "mind-set." It's the she-has-to-be-good-looking-or-at-least-sexy-looking trap. Why? I can understand if you wish to be attached to someone who is responsive to your needs sexually. But, at the risk of sounding trite, since beauty often is in the eye of the beholder, you may want to look more for the kind of beauty that continues even after breasts sag and wrinkles set in. Some women become even more fetching as they age because their inner beauty radiates. Others, who may have been former "prom queens," become sad caricatures of their former selves as their limited personalities shape their lives.

It takes a fairly independent person to get away from the "rich and sexy" trap. It will take determination to overcome the endless media hype of TV, movies, and advertising. But to the victors over this neurosis come some wonderful possibilities. Because most people compete for the "brass ring" of the rich and sexy, for those who are willing to look at new options, there are many wonderful and giving people to choose from.

In this chapter, you have been presented with a multitude of ideas. Through your efforts, you now know the kind of traits which you find attractive and those which turn you off. You have learned what falling in love means. You know that *how* a POS makes you feel about *you* is a crucial test of your compatibility. And finally, you have been presented with new thoughts about age, money, and physical attractiveness. Think about all of this. By now, you should be forming a clear idea of the "color of your paradise."

Chapter Six

The Secret of Being "Attract"-ive

A few months ago, I was having a long-distance telephone conversation with an old friend. As often happens when one talks with a high school chum, we began discussing the same subjects that had preoccupied our thoughts during our high school years. In this case, the subject was what women find attractive in men. Roger insisted that all women seek only good-looking men and aren't interested in those who are neither handsome nor sexy-looking. I disagreed. I argued that women are attracted to men for many reasons, of which looks is not the primary element. But Roger was not to be dissuaded. Even my most cogent arguments, strewn with endless examples of plain and even homely men who have won in love, couldn't shake him from his firm belief in the importance of good looks for success in romance.

Indeed, this had to have been one of the most frustrating conversations I'd ever experienced. Why had Roger been so insistent on maintaining such an irrational view of love? After all, even though he could never pass for Richard Chamberlain's double, he is definitely a pleasant-looking man. And then I remembered. As a teenager, Roger had an acute acne problem, a condition which is a source of unhappiness for millions of teenagers. His father would repeatedly make comments about his son's complexion, almost making Roger feel as if he were to blame for his condition. Seeking advice from dermatologists and even chiropractors, Roger became obsessed with his physical appearance. Now, long after his acne has cleared, he still thinks of himself as unattractive. His non-existent facial scars, with the help of an insensitive parent, have now become deep emotional wounds. So ingrained has Roger's ugly-duckling image become that it affects his relationships with women. Although finding permanent love is one of his primary goals, Roger, now in his mid-thirties, remains unattached.

The major reason for Roger's lack of success with women is his tattered self-image. He has a hard time believing that any worthwhile woman would be attracted to him. As a result, when he meets a woman who *is* interested in him, Roger becomes so possessive, almost leech-like, that he sabotages his chances for developing a healthy relationship. (One good thing has resulted from Roger's preoccupation with acne; he has become a successful dermatologist.)

In the movie, *Annie Hall*, Woody Allen displays similar characteristics. Lacking self-acceptance, he, too, eventually ruins all his relationships with women. He paraphrases Groucho Marx' paradoxical put-down when he says, "Any girl that wants me as her lover couldn't be worthwhile."

It's understandable why so many men and women develop irrational attitudes about love and sex. Relationships with the opposite sex begin in our teens, surely one of the most painfully confusing times in life. Therefore, since we begin to form our concepts of love at this age, we are bound to retain some remnants of our teenage thinking. And what are teenagers preoccupied with? That's right — who is cute, good-looking, gorgeous. No wonder we are all so insecure about our physical appearance.

Of course, the media doesn't help matters any. Just observe the number of times each of us must confront the fantasy of "beautiful people" winning in love and happiness, and you are witnessing the care and feeding of a lucrative neurosis. What's sad is that millions of people "buy into" this kind of propaganda. They get caught up in the pressure to look like one of those who has the "right" look: for women, it's a plentiful bosom; a pair of long, lean legs; a luxurious head of hair; and pearl-white, exquisitely straight teeth — for men, it's muscles like Schwartzenegger's; a moustache like Tom Selleck's; a luxurious head of hair; and pearl-white, exquisitely straight teeth. How we respond to this type of pressure depends on us. For millions, there are two typical responses:

- Spend a small fortune on trying to recreate the latest "approved" look, even if it's unflattering.

- Shrink away from actively seeking any kind of relationship, withdrawing, as it were, from the competition.

How many are obsessed with their looks? If the brisk sales of cosmetics, beauty books, and magazines are any indication, we are a people filled with insecurities. Among the most recent manifestations of the beauty craze are "infomercials" by the likes of Victoria Principal, Cher, and Jane Fonda. When you think about it, I guess these beautiful people *do* have the secret to beauty. All you have to do to look like them is possess their bone structure and the other endowments given them by their

101

"lucky" genes. Seriously, why in the world would anyone buy a beauty book written by someone who is naturally endowed? It really doesn't make a lot of sense. It's like reading a how-to-be-rich book by someone who inherited wealth.

But let's pretend that you have now mastered the art of looking beautiful at all times. Have you solved the problem of loneliness, of finding a suitable mate? Obviously not. Sure, you may turn a few more heads, and that doesn't hurt. But it isn't all that helpful either. Just look at the checkered love life of Liz Taylor, Marlon Brando, and countless other stars, and you see the questionable advantage of physical beauty. (I know, you'd just *love* to be miserable in such grand style. . . How can logic compete with the seductive power of fame?)

So, to quote Joan Rivers, "Grow up!" The I-must-be-good-looking/beautiful-to-make-it-in-love idea is a canard. On its shoulders lies the economic well-being of countless magazines, books, Hollywood promoters, and cosmetic companies. Under its feet are the trampled remains of many worthwhile individuals' self-images.

In order to get hold of this sensitive issue, you need to focus your attention on what's important to you in your campaign. Obviously, beauty for its own sake is not the goal. Rather, you want to attract those with whom you might want to begin a relationship. You want to become a magnet, the object of positive tropism, just as the sun is to the sunflowers. (I know, I know, I'm getting carried away, but what the heck, you get my point.) In that case, I have some good news. As you'll soon see, being attractive is only marginally related to physical beauty And you, my friend, can learn to be irresistibly appealing. All you need to do is to incorporate the following ideas into your life

Seven Ways to Becoming Attractive to Others

One of the definitions of the word, "attract," is "to draw to oneself." Therefore, to be "attract"-ive, we must develop characteristics that draw others to us. What do people find attractive? The following are seven ways in which you can dramatically increase your appeal to others:

I. Personal Hygiene

People are attracted to others who portray a sense of self-worth. You project the way you feel about yourself in a variety of ways. One of them is how you take care of yourself. This may seem elementary to you, but people who respect themselves respect their bodies. They make sure their bodies are clean, their hair is washed regularly, and their breath is sweet-smelling. As powerful an aphrodisiac as good perfume can be, there is nothing as appealing as the just-showered scent of a man or a woman.

II. Outer Appearance

Whether you're male or female, the way you dress and carry yourself says a lot about you. Some people unconsciously wear clothing that makes them appear indistinct. It's almost as though they are trying to hide from the world. Others wear clothes that are so unbecoming and ill-fitting that they are transformed into a walking caricature of themselves. These individuals do not understand that their outer appearance can truly enhance and accentuate their best qualities.

Part of the problem is that few of us see ourselves as we really are. A forty-seven-year-old woman I know still thinks of herself as a teenager. Although she has had three children and has gained at least forty-five pounds since her pom-pom-waving days, she insists on wearing short, pleated skirts and tight-fitting sweaters. I'm sure she thinks her cheerleader outfits are flattering. In fact, they make her look like an ostrich — skinny legs supporting an overripe body. The unfortunate thing is that she is still an attractive woman, and she could, dressed properly, appear quite fetching, even voluptuous. But because she insists on dressing like a teenager, she is missing the opportunity to look like the mature, desirable woman she really is.

Your clothes, your hairdo, even your shoes, are an integral part of the statement you make about yourself. Because most of us do not display ourselves to our best advantage, I recommend that — whether you're a man or a woman — unless you are exceptionally objective about yourself and have an unusually strong sense of style, you seek the help of an expert. In most cases, a salesperson at a clothing store is not what I mean by an expert. Unless these employees are working for an unusual establishment, they have been hired for their sales ability, not their taste. Besides, they will try to sell you what is available in the store, which may or may not be your best choice.

Today, in most cities, you can find a fashion coordinator, or fashion consultant, who will work with you on a personal basis. The very best ones will show you how to look terrific while getting the most out of your shopping dollar. They will assist you in creating the image you want to portray and offer advice on your best colors, makeup, and so forth. (If you prefer to conduct your own independent study, your local bookstore has a growing number of books on this very popular subject.)

III. Self-Acceptance

People are attracted to others who are authentic. Genuine people accept themselves as unique and show pride in who they are — with no apologies. They expect to be liked, just as they expect to like others. This kind of attitude, completely devoid of self-consciousness, is worth emulating. To a large extent, it creates its own self-fulfilling prophecy. Here's an example of such behavior, as written in *Redbook* (see Bibliography) by relationships expert, Judith Viorst:

> I recently met a woman who is fat — not plump, but fat — the kind of woman who should lose thirty pounds, the kind of woman who usually tends to hide in a loose black dress and hopes, at best, that her body won't be noticed. This woman, however, was wearing something flowered and quite low-cut, something that insisted on attention, and it struck me that she simply didn't see herself as "big as a house" — it struck me that she saw herself as. . . voluptuous.
>
> The amazing thing is that, by the end of the evening, I was seeing her as voluptuous too, for she held herself with such pride and such zest and such easy self-assurance that "fat" no longer correctly described her for me. I've watched other women carry off assorted imperfections because they somehow convinced themselves of their physical charms. And I've also watched women much older than I, free of the view that good looks are a function of youth, retain a composed belief in their attractiveness.

Unlike the woman who viewed herself as a teenager, here is another who has learned to take full advantage of her body

105

the way it really is. Instead of clinging to an image that belongs to her past, she has developed self-assurance by convincing herself that she is, today, attractive and desirable. What's the difference between the two women? One's self-image is rooted in self-knowledge, the other in self-delusion.

How you view yourself will determine the kind of relationship you'll develop with others as well as the type of people who become drawn to you. If you like and accept yourself, chances are that others will like you, too. Furthermore, the people who will be drawn to you offer you an unexpected serendipity: They are likely to be those who also have a sense of self-worth.

IV. A Sense of Direction

Unless you are Pygmalion, you will not fall in love with a statue. Unlike this king of Greek mythology, people do not respond to cold beauty. Ultimately, they are attracted to liveliness, positive energy, enthusiasm. How does one develop these qualities? One of the best ways is to create a sense of purpose about at least one aspect of life. It's a fact that goal-oriented individuals, those with an assured sense of direction, possess a special quality — an extra edge that makes them extremely appealing. All winners have this. Their lives are not just based on now but also on the future. They have a plan, and they have a passion about achieving it. Their fervor, their belief in what they do makes them attractive to others.

If you don't have one now, find a project which you can get excited about. It doesn't matter what it is — whether it's your career, a hobby, or charitable involvement — as long as it genuinely gives you a sense of meaning and direction. According to Dr. Viktor Frankl, author of *Man's Search for Meaning* (see Bibliography), the most fulfilled human beings are those who discover their lives are filled with meaning and purpose. Regardless of the source, be it deep religious conviction or the drive to be successful, this sense of meaningfulness allows those who possess it to feel their lives really matter. The happy energy that is released as a result of this belief is strongly appealing.

V. Making Others Feel Special

I once had the experience of going through a reception line to shake the hand of the president of a billion-dollars-a-year corporation. When I reached him and introduced myself, this man, who had already shaken hands with dozens of people in a seemingly endless procession, focused his complete attention on me, just as I'm sure he did with everyone else. As a result, he made me feel important and at ease rather than intimidated. His graciousness was a most attractive quality.

And herein lies the secret to being appealing to others: People are attracted to those who make them feel good about themselves. And people who make others feel accepted are those who take the initiative to make the other person feel comfortable, liked, and appreciated. There is a famous Washington hostess whose parties have always been considered a not-to-be-missed event. This lady, upon first glance, would not be considered to be physically attractive. And yet, she is reputed to have liaisons with some of the most powerful men in the capital. Her secret? Her ability to make others feel supremely appreciated.

Have you ever thought of shyness as a form of selfishness? In a way, it is. Shyness, or self-consciousness, is rooted in self-absorption. It manifests itself when we think about how *we* are feeling, how scared *we* are. If you are skeptical, I recommend that you attend a few meetings of such organizations as Toastmasters, and you'll see how previously shy individuals become powerful orators. This transformation usually occurs once they focus their attention on the needs of their listeners rather than on themselves.

Do you want to be more attractive? Here's something you can do right now. Wherever you are, make a point of being a host instead of a guest. Whenever you are around people, go out of your way to greet them and to make them feel comfortable. If you are at a party (even if you are just a guest) and a new person walks in, make sure that he/she has a drink, is introduced to others, and is made to feel at home. Not only will you be viewed as a leader — as someone who takes charge (because you are stepping out from the crowd) — but you will also meet lots of people who will appreciate your thoughtfulness.

VI. The Art of Listening

One of the most winning traits of attractive people is their ability to listen to others. The world is full of people who want to talk. But it is in short supply of good listeners. Nothing will make you more popular than becoming a good listener. Here are three techniques to help you do that:

1. Use eye contact. Your eyes are the windows to your soul. When you listen to someone else, make sure you look at him/her completely, to the exclusion of the rest of the world. There is nothing more maddening than to talk with someone whose eyes wander all over the place. And yet, many do this frequently.

2. Nod your head sympathetically when others are talking. This helps people feel you care about what they have to say. Nodding your head does not

necessarily mean you agree with what is being said. Rather, it encourages the other person to speak openly and freely.

3.   Ask questions that allow people to know you are listening. Questions that use phrases such as: "Why do you feel this way?" "Please, tell me more. . . ." "What's your opinion of. . . ?" give individuals the opportunity to reveal more of themselves to you. It's rare, indeed, to run into someone with a genuine interest in others.

VII. Flirting

In recent decades, flirting has gone out of favor. The sexual revolution of the past twenty years decreed that the game of pre-sexual anticipation was no longer necessary. But if something serves an important social purpose, we can't simply discard it. Somehow, it finds its way back into civilized society. This is precisely what is happening with flirting. For the purpose of this discussion, I define "flirting" as "playing at the game of love." And I can assure you that, for those who understand its subtlety, learning this "art" can be a tremendous aid in increasing attractiveness.

Let me ask you this question: When men and women meet each other in a non-work-related situation, what is their first concern? Most likely, they would like some indication that their masculinity/femininity has been noticed and, preferably, appreciated. Why do you think women have, historically, found philandering Don Juans attractive? It's because, whatever obvious faults these men possessed, they always allowed their appreciation of a woman's sexuality to be understood. And they made no secret of their admiration. This, in turn, made women feel wanted and desired, often for the first time after a long and tedious marriage.

As part of my research, I made a point of observing singles interacting with each other at parties and other social functions. I witnessed men and women being perfectly nice to each other. And yet, nothing special seemed to happen. Why? Because they acted more like business associates than would-be lovers. There was no I-am-fully-aware-of-your-charms-as-a-man/woman kind of interplay. Much of this is completely understandable. Today, men and women interact at work in situations where one's sexuality has no relevance. It's not easy to change the role back and forth between the work place and the social world. Yet, in spite of this problem, it's important that you learn to flirt again.

How does one flirt? It really is quite simple. A woman is introduced to a man and she thinks to herself, "This guy has really nice eyes." Instead of keeping this discovery to herself, she says to him, "You have wonderful eyes." No big deal. No invitation to the boudoir. Just a simple statement that says, "I find you attractive." Most men (and women) would find this irresistible.

Of course, there are other ways of flirting. Eye contact, an appreciative smile, a reassuring touch on the arm, using a hand to reach up to brush a stray lock of hair from the forehead — all are preludes to developing male/female intimacy. Your enjoyment of the other person's wit or erudition is also a means of capturing attention. Mastering the neglected skill of flirting can help to make you alluring and memorable to someone whom you want to attract.

I hope you now understand how little your "attract"-iveness has to do with natural endowments. You can cultivate your personality and appearance to become as appealing as you choose. I challenge you to accept the opportunity to become the best *you* you can be. Go ahead! Take a look at yourself as you are now, and make whatever changes you deem necessary. Your life may never be quite the same.

Chapter Seven

The Campaign: Part I
Beginning the Search

———————◆———————

If you like to skip around a book to quickly get to the bottom of things, chances are that sooner or later you landed on this chapter. This is the "big" one — the one that explains what the "campaign" is all about. For the rest of you persistent souls who have patiently worked your way through each chapter and who have done the exercises as you went along, more power to you. You will find all your preparatory efforts to be of tremendous value.

Before getting into the heart of the campaign, you need to understand the skeleton. Therefore, you will first be given an overview, and then we'll get into the details. After you've read this and the following two chapters, you should be thoroughly familiar with every aspect of the program.

An Overview (the Skeleton)

Today, many men and women have difficulty when it comes to finding a compatible mate. Once they leave the social laboratory of school where there is constant interaction with other marriageable singles, they are immediately put at a disadvantage. Some postpone marriage because of their commitment to their careers. Others seek new partners after the breakup of an earlier marriage or the death of a spouse. As a result, these men and women are confronted with the reality of looking for a suitable mate in a world dominated by the already-married. The situation is further complicated by the reluctance many feel in dealing with strangers. Horror stories of the *Looking for Mr. Goodbar* type and the epidemic increase in socially communicable diseases such as AIDS have made many turn away from the pickup and the singles bar as a viable method for finding someone. That's why, today, if they are to gain control over the mate-selection process, singles must turn for help to those they already know and trust.

Your friends, relatives, co-workers, and even little-known acquaintances know people who would be suitable candidates for a relationship with you. The problem is that you don't know who these people are. For all practical purposes, they are hidden from you. Therefore, you need to meet with your friends, relatives, and acquaintances to ask for help in reaching these "hidden" singles. (There's a very simple way to do this.) Once you have these referrals, you'll find it easy to call them and set up a time to get together. Why will you find it easy to call? After all, aren't these people total strangers? No, not any longer. When you call a referral, you are calling a friend of a friend — you share a mutual acquaintance.

Sharing this mutual acquaintance makes the magical

difference. It immediately removes you from the "total stranger" category and places you in the inner circle of accepted familiarity. Let me illustrate. Imagine receiving a telephone call from a stranger who tries to sell you a product or being stopped on the street by someone you've never seen before. What's your first reaction? Your pulse quickens, your anxiety level increases, and you become immediately on your guard, prepared to defend yourself against this intruder who dares to invade your privacy. It's an instinctive reaction. Your "territorial wall" has been pierced. All of us have this built-in defense mechanism that makes us fear the unknown, and as part of our drive for self-preservation, we reject any intrusion into our "safe zone."

Once we recognize someone as friendly or familiar to us, we become less anxious, more open. So if a friend calls, we are delighted. And if, by extension, we receive a call from someone who introduces himself or herself as a friend of a friend, we are also delighted.

Advertisers understand and use this human trait to advantage. A shampoo company, for example, will spend tens of millions of dollars acquainting us with its product. Then, when we go to the supermarket, we will choose their friendly and familiar product over an unadvertised and, therefore, unfamiliar brand (even if the unknown product has the same ingredients and costs less). We, in turn, tell our friends about it. And what do our friends do? They immediately go out and buy the product unquestioningly because it was recommended by us.

Now that you understand why calling a referral will be easy and why your call will be welcomed, when you *do* call, suggest that the two of you meet for "a cup of coffee." Stress the informality of the get-together and do not allow it to turn into a date. Why? Because a date, with its obligatory rituals, expense, and romantic expectations would put too much

113

pressure on your new relationship. Besides, it's harder to arrange a date than to schedule a simple get-together at a coffee shop or some other relaxed, neutral location.

Your initial get-together will give both of you an opportunity to see how compatible you are with each other and whether or not you wish to pursue any further relationship. By simply repeating this process of getting referrals from friends and then calling those referrals during a specific ninety-day period, you will meet, one-to-one, face-to-face, a large number of qualified candidates — more than you would normally meet in a year or two. Moreover, by combining both *quantity* of encounters with the *quality* of getting together in this personal and selective manner, you are bound to meet several POS who could end up becoming potential partners for a permanent relationship.

How many POS should you meet in a ninety-day period? That depends, of course, on the amount of time and determination you have committed to your campaign. Naturally, one can't get away from the basic arithmetic of life: The more people you meet in this manner, the more likely you are to find someone in a reasonably short period of time.

Here's what I mean: If you make up your mind to meet two POS through the referral process each week (not an easy task but definitely possible), you will meet a total of twenty-four during a ninety-day period. Let's assume that you disqualify fully half as incompatible. This still leaves twelve candidates with whom you would want to set up another get-together. (This, of course, does not take into account the referrals you might get from those you found incompatible.) Eventually, through the process of further mutual selection, you are going to find four to six POS who are especially suitable — people with whom you have a special rapport. Out of this select group (the creme de la creme, so to speak)

114

of a group of twenty-four POS, you are likely to find *the one* who is as ready and eager as you are to build a special, life-long relationship. At that point, then, your search is over.

As we have already discussed, the ninety-day campaign is derived from key principles used by career counselors and sales trainers and by observing the courting customs of earlier generations. Another way to look at these ideas is to understand them as basic to human nature. In business, we have attached a now-familiar term to the concept of learning the techniques of building new relationships through referrals; it's called "networking." In your campaign, you may want to call it "socializing with a purpose." Whatever the nomenclature, the principle idea is the same: If you want to meet new people, regardless of the reason, the best way to do this is to work through your existing contacts. Why? Because once you are introduced or referred by a mutual acquaintance to someone, you are accepted much more openly than you would be as a stranger.

The Specifics (the Heart)

I. Make a list.

Any people-oriented project must be launched with making a list. And this campaign is no exception. So, it's now time to get out your trusty notebook and start writing a list of all the people you know who live within one hundred miles of you. That's right, one hundred miles. Wouldn't you be willing to drive two hours to meet someone special? The names you put on your list are the people with whom you will be making an appointment to conduct what is called a "referral interview." Who are these people? Close friends? Relatives? Casual acquaintances? There really are no hard and fast rules. Right now, I suggest that you write down anyone and everyone you know. Later on, you will want to sift through your list and choose those who are most likely to know the kind of people you'd want to meet. For example, if the exercises you've just completed show that you like well-organized, meticulous people, try to set a time to see your engineering or scientist friends. They are likely to know colleagues who would probably fit this description. On the other hand, if you are looking for someone with deep spiritual values, see people who are involved in whatever activities you consider to be spiritual.

Now, when it comes to taking direction, most people seek the way of least resistance; it's human nature to look for shortcuts. And since writing lists is not a favorite activity of most people, I've heard some very creative excuses for skipping over this vital step. Here are two of the most common:

1. "I don't need to make a written list. I have a terrific memory. All the names are in my head." Result: Names are forgotten. Also, because the name of one person could act as a memory jogger to scores of other individuals, you are reducing your chances of having a full and complete list at your fingertips.

2. "I don't know too many people, so I don't need to make a list." Result: Because we all know more people than we think, you are omitting a valuable source of names of individuals who can lead you to suitable POS. Remember, we're not only talking about family and close friends but also casual acquaintances.

Don't start off your campaign with excuses or shortcuts. Keep in mind that unless you are a raving genius, you will not remember more than a handful of names at any one time. To paraphrase one of Samuel Goldwyn's famous malapropisms, a mental list isn't worth the paper it's written on. And when it comes to pre-qualifying, most people leave out the most intimidating (the most influential, the ones with the best contacts, the one's who can help the most) people they know.

If you need any further motivation to write your list, just imagine that each name has the potential to lead you to a virtual gold mine of "prospects." You see, every individual on the list lives in his/her own private universe with hundreds of contacts. (Some experts claim that the average person knows about three hundred people.) Since twenty-five percent of the adults today are unmarried, the people on your list are each likely to know scores of singles, thus opening a door to many POS — people who would otherwise remain strangers to you. Imagine further that many of those single people are probably wishing that someone new would call them. (After all, wouldn't you love it if a single friend of someone you know called and proposed a get-together?) As you can easily see, by utilizing this method, the potential for meeting singles of both genders is staggering.

Get the message? To build your campaign on a good foundation of people, right now, start writing names of everyone you can think of. On the following page, you'll find a far-from-comprehensive list of categories of people to help act as a memory jogger. And while you're at it, take a look at your Christmas list, your club-membership rosters, even the yellow pages of the telephone book (you'll be reminded of people as a result of the many professions and businesses listed). Only after you make a long list (at least fifty people) should you feel that you have the raw materials to take the next step.

117

Whom Do You Know?

1. Friends (Include people from your past as well as the present.)
2. Parents
3. Brothers and sisters
4. Grandparents and other relatives
5. Clergy
6. Neighbors
7. Acquaintances
8. People with whom you work (Include all previous jobs.)
9. Your physician, attorney, accountant, banker
10. Members of associations to which you belong
11. POS whom you have dated in the past
12. Same-gender singles with whom you can "trade" information
13. High school and college buddies who live in your area
14. Former teachers or mentors
15. Your children (if they are old enough)

Next, select twenty-four people from your list that you consider the most likely to be of help to you. Here you can consider various factors, such as their socio-economic background (if that's important to you) and the age group of those they might know. For your convenience, write down the telephone number of each person next to his/her name. This makes it more convenient for you because you are ready to call at any time.

II. Set an appointment.

Now that you have a written list, let's talk about scheduling referral interviews with the people you have chosen to call. To risk being obvious, you can reach people in one of three different ways: You can either call, visit, or write. (Carrier pigeons are not very practical.) Most people find calling to be the easiest and most efficient method of setting an appointment.

How you handle your conversation depends on your relationship with the people you are calling. The more familiar you are with each other, the more casual your conversation. But somewhere along the way, you want to tell them the reason for your call, which is to see them in person to "seek their advice about a personal matter."

One common mistake people make is that they tend to discuss the nature of the proposed appointment while on the telephone. What inevitably happens is that one question leads to another and, suddenly, instead of talking face-to-face with that person, they conduct the referral interview on the telephone. So what's the problem with that? Wouldn't that be a time-saver? *NO, NO, NO,* and again, *NO!* Unless you see people in person, you won't get very far. Why? Because most people will give you glib answers and little help over the telephone. Person to person, they will be more inclined to listen intently and to get involved with your project.

So, to labor the same point once more (something I do quite a lot — for your own good), use the telephone merely to set the appointment. Do not allow the conversation to get specific until you meet face-to-face. What should you do if someone insists on knowing the nature of the interview? Simply say that since it's a personal matter you feel uncomfortable discussing it on the telephone. When calling extremely busy people, you can also add that all you need is a half hour of their time.

The location of the referral interview will vary based on your relationship with the person you're calling. If it's a friend or relative, you can meet at an informal place, such as his/her home or a coffee shop. But even when meeting with business people, try to get them away from the office where interruptions are constant and where they are likely to glance impatiently at piles of paperwork. You could suggest a coffee break. Or you could recommend an early-morning breakfast or an appointment right after work.

Last but not least, set an appointment within a reasonably short period of time after your phone call. A good time frame for this is within seven days or less. If the appointment is set further into the future, make sure you confirm it by phone or letter twenty-four to forty-eight hours before you meet.

Let's summarize this section by reviewing the main points to remember in making the initial call:

1. Ask for an appointment to "seek advice about a personal matter."

2. Avoid getting into any further detail.

3. Try to meet at an informal setting with no interruptions.

4. Set and confirm your appointment.

III. Conduct a referral interview.

Your Attitude in the Referral Interview

You should remember at all times that your ultimate goal in setting up referral interviews is to find someone special for a permanent love relationship. And, indeed, your embarking on this campaign displays your commitment to that goal. Yet, paradoxically, the more serious and determined you are, the more essential it is to have a relaxed attitude along the way. Otherwise, you could become so intense that your campaign might backfire. In sports, this process is known as "choking." Basketball players, for instance, can be so bent on scoring that they tighten up their muscles and, as a result, miss an easy shot.

Why do I tell you all this? Because I want you to succeed —I want you to find the love of your life. In the beginning, you're likely to be a bit nervous about setting up your first referral interviews. This is natural. And if you're still not sure of your commitment to the campaign, you may have even decided to test the validity of this method by basing it on your first appointment. This "do or die" attitude toward your referral interview and, for that matter, any other aspect of your campaign can cause you to choke. You know what happens when you and I get too intense about a project. We act unnaturally, sometimes even sabotaging our own efforts. So relax. No interview is a matter of life and death.

There are so many people you can contact that your possibilities of getting referrals are virtually endless. Instead of making each interview too important in your mind, think of it as merely a fact-finding excursion. By all means, develop a sense of positive expectancy about the future meeting of each new person that can result from a referral interview, but don't sweat it, either. After all, the only time any one interview will become overly important in your mind is if it's the only one you have scheduled. Therefore, always have several appointments lined up. A good visualization of the attitude you should develop is to imagine a duck on a pond. On the surface, it is calm — the picture of serenity — but underneath, its feet are paddling like heck!

121

Five Steps to a Successful Referral Interview

You have now set up a referral interview with one of the people on your list. What do you do now? You need to have a strategy that will make it easy for the person with whom you're meeting to help you. For that purpose, let's discuss your referral interview as being composed of five distinct parts. Are you wondering why I recommend this multi-step approach? Why not just tell everyone outright that you want help in meeting new people? You and I both know that's not a good idea. Imagine this: A job hunter bursts into a potential employer's office, grabs him by the collar, and bellows menacingly, "Gimme a job!" Ridiculous, you say? Of course it is. But this scenario is simply an exaggerated example of the type of behavior that puts unnecessary pressure on others. Sure, the job hunter wanted a job. But he failed to use finesse in his approach. The best way to achieve what you want is to take a series of small steps toward your desired goal. Here, then, are the five components of a successful referral interview:

1. *Establish rapport* with the people you contacted. This is not a problem with a friend or close relative, but it's important with less intimate acquaintances. One of the best ways to develop rapport is to *show interest* in them. Make sure you're not so intent on getting your referrals that you omit inquiring about them and their well-being.

2. After spending some time on social chatter (which should be kept short if you're dealing with someone who is pressed for time), *thank the person for seeing you.*

3. *Explain* the reason for the meeting. For example, you may want to say, "My reason for asking to see you is that I need your advice. I've decided to launch a campaign to increase my social circle, especially of other singles. Because you are (here, give them a genuine compliment that fits them), I thought that you would be an excellent person to give me some ideas on how I should go about meeting new people."

Notice that at this point you are not yet asking for names of other singles. Why? Because you want to proceed gradually; you don't want to pressure them. Very often, they will start giving you names without prompting. And by not putting them on the spot, you are giving them the opportunity to become involved naturally.

Note: Each of us has a unique reason why we are interested in increasing our circle of acquaintances. When you meet with the people on your list, you can personalize your reason. For example, if you have been divorced recently, you can tell people that you are now "ready to get out of your cocoon and rebuild your social life." Sylvia, a widow, told her friends that she wanted to meet new people in order to renew her sense of excitement about living. She was introduced by her deceased husband's business partner to a man whose wife had just died a year earlier. They have been inseparable ever since. Gary, a sales representative for a jeans manufacturer, was transferred to Phoenix, where he knew no one. After he became settled in his new home, he approached several clergymen of his faith about his desire to meet singles with a similar background to his. According to Gary, "It will take me three months just to meet all the women whose names I was given."

4. *Listen* to the advice you are given. You may get some great ideas. And, as we discussed, many people will start coming up with names of people they think you should meet. After awhile, if the person doesn't come out with an "As a matter of fact, you ought to meet. . ." kind of statement, ask outright, "Would you know of any single people, either male or female, that I should meet?" (As you'll soon see, you will benefit from meeting both POS and people of the same sex.) If you get a positive response, note the name, address, and telephone number of each person. (Try for several.) Make sure to ask questions about each of the people. The more information you have, the better. For example, if someone says to you, "You ought to meet my nephew, John," you can respond by saying, "Great, tell me about him." This way, you can get to know quite a bit about John, which will allow you to decide if you want to meet him. And if you do decide to meet, you will be able to relate to him more easily.

Sometimes, people will not be able to think of anyone on the spot. In that case, try to jog their memory by asking them about whom they might know from work, social activities, and so on. Finally, if they are still not able to offer you any names, ask their permission to call within two or three days to see if they might have thought of a few people.

5. *Ask for permission* to keep them informed of your progress. Not only will they appreciate this but they will also be complimented. By staying in touch, people will feel as though they have a stake in your success. As time goes by, some of them will even think of new people for you to meet. As a result, you will have a veritable network of helpers actively looking for suitable people for you. This is exactly what happened to Cathy, a twenty-nine-year-old mother of two who was determined not to raise her children alone. She had so many of her friends looking for her that she ended up meeting lots of men in a short period of time. She is now married to Dean, a self-employed builder/contractor, whom she dated for a year and a half.

Another way to keep people interested in your campaign is to send them a personalized thank-you note within twenty-four hours of meeting with them. This simple follow-up is much more than just exercising good manners. It is an excellent way to ensure that you will be remembered. Now, when your friends with whom you had referral interviews run across eligible singles, they will automatically think of you. You can also reiterate in your thank-you note that you will be in touch from time to time.

Note: In our age, when fewer and fewer people are in the habit of writing letters, this step is frequently overlooked. Yet, your written thanks is an essential part of your campaign.

Getting Referrals from Singles

If you are conducting a referral interview with another unattached single, there is one more thing for you to consider. He/she will also be interested in getting some new ideas on how to meet POS. Therefore, think of this interview as more of an exchange of information. The other single is likely to be just as interested in meeting new people as you are. So share your knowledge. Undoubtedly, you know some people or activities that he/she will want to know about. This kind of free exchange of information will be of use to you whenever you meet with other singles with whom you have no desire to become romantically involved. The more you are willing to share, the more others will want to share with you.

Now that You Have Some Names. . .

Many of your referral interviews will result in at least one or even many names of POS. Others will yield a name or two of people of the same sex (PSS). Either way, you are succeeding in your campaign. You now have the names of other singles to call who are a recommendation from a mutual acquaintance. This is an opportunity for real contact with new people whom you did not know before. And because you learned something about these people in your referral interviews, you have a distinct advantage.

Should you be given the name of a PSS, don't be disappointed. In fact, you should look forward to developing new relationships with others who share your experience. There are even some wonderful advantages. Linda, a thirty-six-year-old attorney, regularly tries to meet other women of her general age and background. Aside from some wonderful friendships that have developed, she has found these women

126

to be a good source of information. She regularly exchanges names of men with them. As she says, "Just because I haven't continued a relationship with a guy doesn't mean that someone else won't find him irresistible."

Now, let's review the essential steps of the referral interview:

1. Establish rapport with those you meet.

2. Thank them for seeing you.

3. Explain the reason for the meeting.

4. Seek advice on conducting your campaign and ask for names of those you should meet.

5. Get permission to keep them involved in your campaign by staying in touch, and send a thank-you note within twenty-four hours after each interview.

One final word: If you are at all hesitant about calling people to set up referral interviews because you don't want to bother them, remember this: Most people genuinely enjoy helping others. When you seek their advice, you are paying them a high compliment. As a result, you are giving almost as much as you are receiving.

IV. Set up a get-together (rendezvous).

The Phone Call

Once you receive the name of another single, call right away. You may be tempted to procrastinate (that old fear-of-being-rejected demon), but call anyway within a day or two. Why? Because you want to meet the new person while you are still enthusiastic and while the details of your referral interview are still fresh in your mind.

In order to help you visualize calling a referral, I have included a sample script of a telephone call to a new contact:

Mary: Hello, John?

John: Speaking.

Mary: Hi! My name is Mary, and I'm a friend of Ralph Schmidt.

John: Oh, hi.

Mary: Listen, John, I realize that we don't know each other, but Ralph spoke very highly of you and recommended that I give you a call. I was wondering if you would be open to meeting sometime for a cup of coffee?

John: Sure, I'd love to. When did you have in mind?

Mary: How about after work? What afternoon is good for you?

John: Thursday at five looks good.

Mary: Terrific, why don't we meet at the coffee shop at the Hilton?

John: Sounds good, I'll see you on Thursday.

Mary: See you then. Oh, by the way, I'll be wearing a blue outfit. Goodbye.

Notice how little time the whole interchange took. Certainly, an actual phone call could include some more "fluff." For example, John could have asked about Ralph's well-being, or Mary could have taken more time to get to the reason for the call. But even with a more florid approach, the whole conversation should take only a few minutes. Remember, your goal on the phone is simply to set a time for a get-together (from now on, we'll call this "rendezvous" — it sounds nicer), so keep it short.

In spite of the apparent simplicity of the conversation between Mary and John, the words used are carefully chosen. In fact, the whole sequence of the conversation is geared toward Mary's achieving the goal of setting up a rendezvous with John.

The Psychology of Calling

Let's take a look at the psychology behind Mary's phone call:

1. "My name is Mary, and I'm a friend of Ralph Schmidt." Here, Mary introduces herself and quickly establishes the connection between John and her, namely, Ralph Schmidt. Ralph's familiar name immediately gives the conversation a friendly air.

2. "I realize that we don't know each other." Here, Mary is using the technique of stating the objection. John could be wondering, "What does she want from me?" By stating this objection frankly, Mary shows her openness, thus removing any residue of mistrust.

3. "Ralph spoke very highly of you and recommended that I give you a call." Here, Mary is doing two things. First, she gives John a sincere compliment, which should please him. Second, she implies that she is simply complying with Ralph's suggestion that "I give you a call." This tactic allows Mary to deal from a position of strength. It eliminates any feeling that Mary is "chasing" him or that he would be doing her a favor by meeting with her. (Besides, if he is so highly thought of by Ralph, he'd better rise to his chivalrous best.)

4. "I was wondering whether you would be open to meeting sometime for a cup of coffee?" This sentence is packed with choice words. The word, "open," creates a friendly, non-threatening atmosphere. Used as it is, Mary is making it almost impossible for John to say no. After all, if he replies negatively to this question, John is, in effect, saying that he is "closed." The phrase, "cup of coffee," also has an important reason behind it: It communicates to John a neutral meeting, not a date. In effect, it says, "There are no expectations or strings attached. Neither one of us is making any commitment or is under any obligation."

5. "How about after work? What afternoon is good for you?" Again, Mary is reiterating the neutrality of the rendezvous. She's making it sound relaxed and casual. In this particular case, since they both work downtown, she is recommending that they meet right after work, a time that is mutually convenient. Furthermore, by referring to the afternoon, she is indicating a non-date environment.

Notice, also, how Mary is asking John to tell her which afternoon *he* is available. This forces John to commit himself. If, instead, Mary had proposed a definite time by saying, "How about Wednesday afternoon?" and John had been busy, she would have lost the initiative by having to propose another time — a poor tactic, indeed. This would have also made it appear that John's time is more valuable than Mary's. Finally, notice how Mary keeps asking the questions. By doing this, she is gently guiding the conversation to the desired result; she's the one in control. In addition, she is choosing in advance the location she considers best.

Here's a good place to answer a frequently raised objection. Many people resent the employment of any strategy when it comes to love. The idea that one would consciously apply negotiation techniques in developing a relationship seems downright sacrilegious to them. But I ask you, if negotiating is part of every aspect of life, from getting a raise in salary to persuading your three-year-old to go to bed, why should love be exempted? Besides, at this early stage of the game, love isn't even a factor. All you are doing is arranging to meet someone new. And believe me when I say that the attitude you portray and the words you choose, starting with your initial phone call, can either help or hinder your chances for success.

Note: Although the example above depicts a woman calling a man, this technique would work equally well when a man calls a woman. For that matter, there would be little difference even if you were calling a PSS instead of a POS.

The Gender Gap

Let's face it. One of the barriers to male/female relationships in the post-feminist-revolution era is that the old courting rules don't make sense anymore. And yet, there have emerged few new rules to replace the old ones. As in any post-revolutionary time, there is a period of social confusion; nobody seems to know quite how to behave. Is it any wonder, then, that books on etiquette are sprouting everywhere? It's as if everyone wants to be told what to do and how to do it.

I bring all this to your attention because, in this book, I have treated men and women equally. Members of both sexes are expected to embark on their campaign to find love. Furthermore, both men and women are expected to make phone calls to new POS. And yet, I know that for many women the old traditions of courting and dating are still a powerful force. The rational mind may, figuratively, stand up for equality of the sexes, yet the emotional underpinning quickly sits down when it comes to taking direct action to achieve a lasting relationship. Specifically, I am talking about the question of who calls whom. I personally know several women, some of whom are enthusiastic feminists, who are still uncomfortable in taking the initiative when it comes to calling a man.

Does any of this apply to you? Are you still reluctant to call a man concerning a rendezvous? Then you need to overcome your hesitancy. You simply cannot have it both ways. If you want to find your ideal mate, then you should realize that men and women *both* are bewildered by all the changes in the male/female social code. As a result of the general confusion about roles, men have encountered so many different attitudes in women that many are downright reluctant to initiate any action. In a way, we have what amounts to a standoff between the sexes. Millions of women wouldn't think of calling men, and millions of men are too intimidated to call women.

I believe that most men would be absolutely delighted if a woman called them and proposed a rendezvous. It would be a positive statement that simply affirms the mutual responsibility both share toward any relationship. The question of who calls whom should become irrelevant. Quite simply, if you are committed to finding the love of your life, you should expect to take the initiative and make something happen regardless of your gender.

The Rendezvous: Attitudes and Goals

Once you have called and set an appointment with a POS, you have reached a milestone. You now own the knowledge of how you can meet an endless variety of new people. But there is much more value in this kind of encounter than simply meeting a large number of singles. When you meet with someone as a result of a referral interview, over a cup of coffee, you are spending quality time together in an environment that allows both of you to see each other as real human beings. This is in sharp contrast to most situations where strangers treat each other like objects. Just think of the typical party atmosphere — loud music, the obnoxious behavior of intoxicated individuals, no chance for intimate conversation. Add to that the tendency to see potential mates as sex objects. Hardly a conducive atmosphere for a person to make real contact with another!

First dates aren't much better. You and your companion are preoccupied with so many details: the desire to make a positive first impression, remembering how to get to the theatre, thinking about the cost of the meal, worrying over who should pay for it, being nervous about pronouncing the French wine correctly, and finally, wondering if you should end the evening in bed. It's like driving a car for the first time — you're so busy trying to avoid an accident there's no time to enjoy the scenery.

But when you are meeting for a cup of coffee instead of going on a date, there's an air of simplicity about the event. It's a casual meeting, no strings attached. You are simply exchanging ideas and, possibly, finding areas of mutual interest. There are few distractions — just two people meeting each other for friendly conversation. And that's the real key: You have an opportunity for meeting another human being away from the hype. This, in turn, gives you the chance to express your uniqueness while discovering the special qualities of your new friend.

What you want to accomplish at a rendezvous depends on whether you are meeting with a PSS or a POS. If you were referred to a PSS, your goals are:

1. To create friendship and to be introduced into a new social world. Your new friend may invite you to join a new organization, to attend a concert, to go bicycling, or to meet an eligible brother or sister.

2. To exchange information. You may have gone out with a POS who just might be attractive to your new friend, and vice versa. Exchanging this kind of information can be productive for both of you.

There are few things in life that are as rewarding as meeting a new friend. At the very least, you have developed a new contact and opened a door to new friendships. So you see, you are already winning.

When meeting with a POS, it is inevitable that you will be more on your toes. After all, you are on a campaign to find the love of your life, and maybe, just maybe, he/she is that special person. It is precisely because of this possibility that I'd like to warn you to not change your attitude about your rendezvous. Remember, this is simply a preliminary get-together with another human being, a chance to get to know someone better. If you put too much expectation into this encounter, you could be disappointed. Fantasizing, anticipating too much, is destructive. It can increase your frustration if nothing special happens. Make an attempt to be as unexpecting about the meeting as possible. This doesn't mean that you shouldn't be enthusiastic about the possibility of finding a potential mate or delighted once you meet someone who interests you. On the contrary. Just remember that the process of turning a casual new acquaintance into a candidate for a serious love relationship takes time. Over-eagerness can be a turn-off.

If You Meet the "Wrong" Person. . .

Okay, you are now meeting your rendezvous partner. As you greet each other, you can already tell that this is going to be a *long* half hour. There is very little about your "friend" that you like. What to do? Immediately turn this meeting into a referral interview. Explain that you are trying to meet singles and to make new friends (stress the platonic nature of the word) and that because his/her name was given to you, you wanted to meet. Keep asking questions about his/her work and interests. But gradually, shift the conversation by asking, "By the way, since I'm trying to meet as many singles as possible, I was wondering if you can think of other men and women that I should meet?" You never know, this person just might have a terrific roommate, right? So, even though it is said that you can't squeeze blood out of a turnip (an awful expression), you may get some great referrals out of a not-so-hot POS. The key is to keep asking for referrals

135

and to contact them, just as you have learned in the script. Only those who keep digging are likely to find the hidden gold.

Note: Sometimes, when meeting POS in this fashion, you might be immediately attracted to someone, and at other times you may be totally unimpressed. I hope you will allow yourself to have a bit of a wait-and-see-attitude about everyone you meet. Try to see the best in the other person —seek out his/her areas of greatest strength and interest. And unless he or she is clearly not compatible with you, be patient. You never know, you just may end up discovering a truly special person after all.

To summarize this chapter, here are the steps you need to take to launch your campaign:

Step I: Make a list of people to approach for referrals.

Step II: Set an appointment to see those people.

Step III: Conduct a referral interview with the goal of getting names of other singles.

Step IV: Set an appointment with your referrals for an informal rendezvous "for a cup of coffee."

How does one develop rapport during the rendezvous? That's what Part II of the campaign is all about.

Chapter Eight

The Campaign: Part II
Getting to Know Each Other
(the Rendezvous)

———————◆———————

The moment has come. As a result of your referral interview and proper follow-up, you were given the name of a POS. You called and set up a get-together "for a cup of coffee and a chat." And *Bingo!* Unlike other less successful encounters, you hit it off! It doesn't really matter what led to your meeting. Perhaps he or she is a relative of one of the people on your referral interview list, or maybe you had to dig further — this person being a referral from a referral (a PSS who exchanged names with you or a POS who introduced you to his/her roommate). The fact is that you are winning. You have uncovered a previously "hidden" single, one with whom you could possibly develop a lasting relationship.

After your initial enthusiasm subsides, you may experience a different emotion: anxiety. The fact is that, invariably, success exacts its toll. Once you begin the task of building a relationship, the stakes get higher. A person who was previously a total stranger is now a candidate for intimacy. You begin to care. You want to make sure that the sparks of mutual attraction will ignite into a burning flame. You feel anxious. Your mind ruminates with the persistent and nagging thought, "Now, how do I keep this going?"

I, too, have experienced this feeling several times. The first time I recall feeling this way was on my first date, when I was fourteen. Having newly arrived in this country, my knowledge of English was limited. But I desperately wanted to go out with Valerie, one of the most popular girls in my class. Mustering all my courage, I finally called and invited her on a date, which she, to my great surprise, accepted. My initial excitement quickly turned to panic. "What do I say to her? What do people talk about for four hours? Suppose she makes fun of my accent?" were some of the thoughts racing through my mind. Finally, I came up with what I thought to be a brilliant solution. I took Valerie to a three-hour movie, after which we stopped at a hamburger joint that had a jukebox. Since Valerie loved the Beatles, I kept feeding the machine with quarters. Between bites of her sandwich and fries and sips of her milk shake, Valerie kept humming away while tapping her feet to the rhythm of the music. I received a reprieve. I didn't have to think of anything to talk about. As you may have guessed, this evening out did not stimulate everlasting devotion. In fact, I have no doubt that thoughts of me were erased from Valerie's mind the moment the door to her parents' house closed behind her.

Are you also concerned about your ability to carry on a conversation? Do you think of yourself as shy? Then I have some good news for you. You really don't need to be a brilliant conversationalist in order to communicate effectively with a POS. No one expects you to match the oratorical brilliance of a Lady Astor or a William F. Buckley. Rather than potent elocution skills, you need to have an understanding of people. Once you acquire this insight, you will use it to develop rapport and intimacy with others. That's why much of this chapter is devoted to explaining how to develop greater closeness and caring between two individuals. As you read the following pages, you'll notice that I've combined broad principles with very specific and detailed instructions. Both are necessary for your success.

Before going any further, let's cover what your initial goals should be when meeting someone new at a rendezvous. They are:

1.   To get to know the person you are meeting and to discover if, indeed, you have important areas of common interest or agreement.

2.   To develop rapport by subtly revealing your uniqueness.

3.   To create, if you find the other person attractive, the kind of atmosphere that will gradually lead both of you toward greater intimacy.

Intimacy — a Gradual Process

In his book, *Intimate Behaviour* (see Bibliography), Desmond Morris describes a hierarchy of interactions between men and women who are building a relationship. His studies led him to observe that there is a fairly predictable ritual that men and women go through in the process of developing greater intimacy. (He counts twelve steps from first glimpse to sexual union.)

How is this significant to your understanding of the rendezvous? From the moment you lay eyes on each other, your relationship with the other person begins. In fact, because first impressions are often indelible, your initial actions normally set the tone for the rest of the rendezvous. Therefore, the importance of the beginning few moments upon first meeting a possible love candidate cannot be overstated. If your persona communicates a certain naturalness, a sense of relaxed confidence, you will portray a most attractive image. On the other hand, if you appear anxious and self-conscious, you will make your counterpart feel ill-at-ease.

In a way, the ritual people go through to get to know each other is similar to the peeling of an onion. We all have many layers of "realness." There is the public us, the one we tell about in a resume. On the other extreme, there is our inner child, the deeply hidden part of us that we don't often reveal, even to ourselves. For a relationship between two people to literally unfold, a gradual process must occur that allows men and women to reveal themselves to each other one step at a time. Think of it this way: Two strangers are meeting each other for the very first time. If they discover enough in common, they will gradually build bonds of trust that will allow them, over a period of several days or even several years, to reveal more of themselves. (There is never a set agenda for the growth of intimacy and love.)

Too Closed, Too Open

I have had many women tell me how difficult it is for them to get to know some men. (I have also known women who would make a sphynx appear talkative.) And, indeed, people who are afraid to reveal themselves have difficulty in developing intimacy. As one woman said: "Even after Jack and I went out for two months, I still felt as if I were prying whenever I asked him about his past. That guy was impossible to get to know."

But as destructive as is the emotional barrier that "closed" people erect, there is the opposite phenomenon of being too open, too soon. In recent years, there has been a new fad sweeping the nation. It's a variation on the theme of "true confessions." There are those who are more than eager to reveal every facet of their lives to anyone who might listen. These people practice a let-it-all-hang-out philosophy, having become enamored with the latest Hollywood fad of post-psychotherapy "confessions," as practiced on afternoon TV talk shows. This penchant for emotional exhibitionism becomes a turn-off to those with even a modicum of propriety and privacy about their lives.

In other words, take it easy. Leave some mystery in your relationship. You don't have to divulge everything there is to know about yourself during your first encounter. Allow the onion-peeling process to proceed naturally. Far too often, potentially wonderful relationships are cut off when one of the people involved feels overwhelmed by it all. If you've ever had a great date, after which your new friend didn't call (and who hasn't?), chances are that this is what happened. As Maxine Schnall writes in *Every Woman Can Be Adored* (see Bibliography), "Nothing will stand you in better stead than the ability to let a relationship evolve until you know that it's this (person) you want. . . ."

Self-Respect, the Universal Desire

Recently, there has been much talk by both men and women about their need for "self-expression." It's as if, in our crowded world, people want to hear the sound of their own voices, if just to make sure they're really alive. No one can argue with this need. To challenge self-expression would be like questioning motherhood or the value of democracy. Yet, too often, this thirst for self-expression is proclaimed most loudly by those who view each encounter with another human being as their chance for a "me, me, me" monologue or what Baxter and Corinne Geeting, authors of *How to Listen Assertively* (see Bibliography), call "oral hemophilia."

Some of this is understandable. Living in seclusion as they often do, many people, and singles in particular, have a rare opportunity to share their thoughts with others. What is tragically not understood by those who wallow in their oratorical orgies is that their need to talk incessantly is sabotaging their chance at intimacy with anyone who has a healthy self-image. And further, because they are invariably trying to prove something with their talk, they are laying siege to their hapless listeners, who become victims of this neurotic need to assert an often-battered ego.

Let me give you an example. Not so long ago, I had lunch with an attorney over a potential business deal. Because he was pressed for time, he asked me to stay an extra day in the city so that we could "really get acquainted." In fact, he invited me to join him for a polo game. I agreed to remain, hoping to further discuss my business proposal. What transpired was one of the most brutal non-violent sessions I have ever experienced. From the moment this person picked me up at my hotel, he talked incessantly about himself, his successes, his cars, his houses, his . . ., well, you get the message. By the end of the day, when I was limply dropped off at my hotel, I had developed the most excruciating headache and a most unbenevolent feeling toward this neurotic who raped my mind and used me as his audience.

My point is this: Any interchange between two individuals must have a balance between give and take. Both parties must feel they are respected and considered. When you meet with people, make sure they feel that you are really listening to what they have to say. In short, don't behave like the famous producer (or was it a movie star?) who, after two hours of talking about his latest success, finally noticing the drooping eyelids of his date, said, "Enough about me. What did *you* think of my last movie?"

In his book, *How to Have Confidence and Power in Dealing with People* (see Bibliography), Les Giblin says it best when he writes:

> No human being is self-sufficient. Each of us needs things that other people have to offer. You have things that other people need. All our dealings with other people are based upon these needs. There are only three basic ways in which we deal with other people:
>
> 1. You can take what you need from the other fellow by force, threats, intimidation, or by outsmarting him. Although criminals naturally fall in this category, many respectable people employ this method in more subtle ways.
>
> 2. You can become a human relations beggar, and beg other people to give you the things you want. This submissive type of personality makes a deal with other people: "I won't assert myself in any way or cause you any trouble, and in return you be nice to me."
>
> 3. You can operate upon a basis of fair exchange or give-and-take. You make it your business to give other people things they want and need, and invariably they will turn around and give you things you need.

What do you suppose most people need from others? In our overcrowded world, there is one desire which is universal. This quiet but ubiquitous need tugs at everyone's heart. It is a silent cry which says, "I want to feel important — that what I am and what I do matters." Most of us, regardless of what we do, need validation from others. Therefore, if you treat those you meet at your rendezvous with the respect and understanding they need, you will find that they, too, will listen to you and will want to know you better.

Yes, we are all egoists. Our projects and our problems are of much greater interest to us than to anyone else. Therefore, in a world where most people want to talk about themselves, who do you think is in most demand? That's right, the person who can put the limelight on others by being a good listener.

When Justice Oliver Wendell Holmes was asked to give advice on how to get along with people, he wrote:

> To be able to listen to others in a sympathetic and understanding manner is perhaps the most effective mechanism in the world for getting along with people and tying up their friendship for good. Too few people practice the "white magic" of being good listeners.

Your Rendezvous: Steps Toward Intimacy

So much for the broad principles for conducting your get-together. Now, let's get specific by going step by step through the initial stages of the rendezvous. This is important because the first steps are usually the most awkward. Your relationship begins as soon as you see each other. Therefore, let's take a look at your rendezvous with a potentially desirable POS from the perspective of making your first appearance as effective as possible.

The First Visual Contact

Our first impressions are the most memorable. Therefore, the impression you initially make is of tremendous importance to the overall success of each rendezvous.

There are several aspects involved with the first visual contact. These consist of your physical appearance, your walk, eye contact, and, finally, your smile. Before going any further, however, I must tell you that I have no intention of making any comments on the proper way to dress. Why? First of all, I have no knowledge of what image you wish to portray, so I would never be so presumptuous as to advise you on your attire. Second, I could never hope to compete with the clothing experts. The bookstores are filled with books giving professional advice on this subject. You can learn how to dress for business success, how to become color-coordinated, or how to dress like royalty on a shoe-string. I leave any further discussion to these sartorial sages who have spent time researching, compiling, and writing about this popular topic. I would only say this: No matter what, make sure you allow yourself to be the best *you* that you can be. Even if you don't attach much importance to clothing, don't allow this attitude to detract from your overall chances for success. Remember, your clothing is an integral part of *your* total image.

Physical Appearance

Do you recall the telephone conversation script (from the previous chapter) that describes how to set up a rendezvous? There, Mary made a point of telling John how to find her. ("I'll be wearing a blue outfit.") For the moment, let's assume that you are Mary. Because you know that the very first impression you'll make is a visual one, you have several

145

choices before you. First, you get to select the location. You may choose a dimly lit lounge or a brightly lit coffee shop. It all depends on whether you want to be seen in broad daylight or whether you prefer to be seen in more subdued lighting. Second, you can decide whether you want to arrive slightly early or a little late. Why would that matter? Simply because if you are already seated when John comes, if you want to de-emphasize your body, you can. On the other hand, if you want to make an "entrance," you can walk toward John (who, we hope, described himself over the telephone) in your fullest glory.

Earlier, I urged you to be proud of who you are and to accept yourself, regardless of your weight, height, or any other potential "blemishes." However, if at this point you are still unsure of your physical appearance, you are now aware of two strategies to help you reduce any negative impression made by your physique: choosing a dimly lit location for the rendezvous and arriving early so that you can already be seated when the other person arrives.

Your Walk

If you have decided to make an entrance, be sure that you understand the importance of your walk. To a large degree, your walk expresses your mental attitude. A person who is weighted down with the world's problems scuffles around with drooping shoulders and no energy. On the other hand, a person can convey confidence by walking a bit faster than most, head held high, shoulders drawn back. So, when you greet John, make sure you walk toward him with good posture and plenty of energy.

Eye Contact

Eye contact is the most powerful and instantaneous way for people to achieve mutual recognition. Unfortunately, many have difficulty looking directly into another person's eyes. Instead of offering a firm, friendly gaze, they tend to avert their eyes away from the other individual.

When you meet John, make sure your eyes lock for a few seconds. This doesn't mean that you want to "stare him down." (This isn't showdown at the O.K. Corral.) Just let your eyes linger long enough for both of you to acknowledge each other.

Your Smile

A fundamental part of your first visual contact is your smile. Most people are self-conscious and a bit inhibited when they meet someone new. As a result, they smile a mechanical smile, one that projects little of themselves. How unfortunate, since a smile is one of the most magical aspects of an individual's personality. A broad, warm, from-way-down-deep smile can, like nothing else, set the tone for your rendezvous. When you smile deeply and warmly, you are conveying the message of friendliness and openness, an irresistible combination. In effect, you're saying, "I'm happy that we're meeting, and I look forward to a pleasant time." This sets a wonderful tone for your encounter.

How is *your* smile? Are you a bit out of practice? Then why don't you start learning the art of smiling? Each morning, as part of your daily ritual, practice smiling in front of the mirror. It will probably be the single most important beauty treatment you could give yourself. Nickie, a pianist in her mid-forties, is considered by many to be an attractive lady. In fact, her features are quite plain. But Nickie has

147

developed such a wonderful smile that she attracts people to her. It seems that everyone wants to bask in her inviting countenance.

There is yet another reason you should smile broadly. John is probably as nervous as you are. He is wondering if you will like him. Therefore, your welcoming smile will ease his discomfort. Since everyone likes to be accepted, John will be more likely to reciprocate your friendliness.

The Greeting

The next step toward intimacy is your greeting. In addition to the use of eye contact, which we've already discussed, there are two elements in your greeting that are worth discussing. They are your verbal introductions and your handshake.

Verbal Introductions

The way you use your voice is part of the overall image you create. A frightened, tentative "Hello" will make you appear, not surprisingly, frightened and tentative. On the other hand, a more assertive introduction will instill more confidence in those you're meeting. You don't have to be fancy. A simple "Hi, John. I'm Mary" said in a confident, friendly manner will do just fine.

Your Handshake

Are you a bone crusher, or are you a dead fish? Please, I'm not trying to insult you. What I have described here are two types of handshakes that, according to experts, adversely influence the opinion others will hold of you. A weak handshake often connotes a weak self-image, while a pulverizing handshake, in addition to inflicting pain, signifies

148

that someone is "trying to prove something." The best handshake is firm, with just enough squeeze in it to say, "I'm glad to meet you."

Practice Makes Perfect

In chapter three, I described the power of visualization. Here is a way you can use visualization to prepare for your rendezvous with a POS: Utilizing all the points in this section on making a positive first impression, visualize yourself going through the preliminary process of your meeting, from the moment you spot him/her to the time you greet each other. Do this several times, especially if you are somewhat apprehensive about meeting strangers.

Once you visualize this sequence in your mind, do a few actual run-throughs in the privacy of your room. Practice smiling warmly. Walk energetically toward your imaginary friend with your hand extended, ready for a handshake. Choose an object in the room and, imagining it to be the face of the other person, practice focusing your eyes on it. You may feel a bit awkward, even silly. But the reward of a few dry runs like this will be your ease and confidence when the real event occurs.

Getting to Know Each Other

In the following section, we'll explore what can happen once your rendezvous gets on its way. However, before we begin the discussion of what to talk about and how to say it, I'd like to first discuss what subjects you should avoid in an initial meeting or, for that matter, any time you begin a new relationship.

Five Subjects to Avoid at Your Rendezvous

1. Avoid sexist generalities. Often, in a misdirected attempt to protect themselves against disappointments, men and women will rail against the opposite sex. This kind of behavior can be detected as soon as a statement is made that begins with, "The trouble with men/women is. . ." Actually, generalities about either gender come off as shrill. They add an air of stridency and narrow-mindedness to any discussion, and, like all prejudices, they build walls instead of bridges.

2. Avoid derogatory remarks about former spouses or lovers. This may seem so obvious to you, yet, over and over again, formerly attached singles use dates as a forum to vent their anger about past relationships that didn't work out. Your rendezvous is not a therapy session and is, therefore, a poor place for a diatribe against your former mate. In addition to imposing on your listener, it reflects badly on you. After all, you chose the turkey in the first place.

3. Avoid discussing intimate information about a former relationship. As part of the previously mentioned fad to "tell all," some people take the liberty of discussing intimate details about former lovers. Any sensitive person listening to this will undoubtedly wonder, "If he is telling me all this about her, what will he say to others about me?"

4. Avoid a discussion of health problems. Your rendezvous is not the time to play General Hospital. Nor is it a place to give an "organ" recital ("I have a bad back. . . I have sinus problems. . ." and so on). There is nothing more boring, not to mention sexually uninviting, than individuals who insist on discussing their aches and pains.

5. In general, avoid complaining. There is a saying: "You can have my sympathy or my respect, but you can't have both." If your quest is for a healthy relationship between two equals, avoid any tendency to appeal to someone else's sympathy. If, in the past, you developed the habit of manipulating others to feel sorry for you, you need to carefully examine this tendency. It could be a contributing factor as to why you haven't yet found a fulfilling relationship.

Goals

One of the exciting aspects of any rendezvous with a new acquaintance is that you don't know what will transpire. At a certain point, a successful conversation assumes its own form and "takes off." It would, therefore, be unproductive to try to recreate an imaginary conversation. Nevertheless, regardless of what form your conversation takes, you should remain at all times completely aware of your goals when you first meet someone. In fact, let's review the three objectives of each rendezvous:

1. To get to know the person you are meeting and to discover if, indeed, you have important areas of common interest or agreement.

2. To develop rapport by subtly revealing your uniqueness.

3. To create, if you choose, the kind of atmosphere that will lead both of you gradually toward greater intimacy.

Openers

One of the most often disparaged forms of human communication is small talk. And yet, this lowly form of interaction plays an essential role in the evolution toward intimacy. As Desmond Morris writes (see Bibliography):

> Invariably, the initial comments will concern trivia. It is rare at this stage to make any direct references to the true mood of the speakers.This small talk permits the reception of a further set of signals, this time to the ear instead of the eye. Dialect, tone of voice, accent, mode of verbal thinking, and use of vocabulary permits a whole new range of units of information to be fed into the brain.

In addition to providing more information about each other, small talk is part of the onion-peeling process we discussed earlier. It allows you and the POS facing you to become more comfortable with each other. It really doesn't matter which of the everyday subjects you "small-talk" about —except for this: Avoid setting a complaining, whiny tone to the conversation. Even if you choose to mention that your car battery died that morning, you can relate this with a smile, laughing at life's misadventures instead of being overwhelmed by them. The difference is obvious.

152

Getting to the Purpose of the Rendezvous

After a certain amount of small talk, it will be necessary for you to state the reason for your meeting. It's important that you think about it, and prepare a script that you feel comfortable with. The variations are endless. Here's an example of what you could say:

"John, I really want to thank you for meeting with me. (Here, John will probably respond.) Actually, I must confess to you that I was a bit nervous calling someone I've never met before. But because Ralph Schmidt spoke so highly of you, I decided to take the chance and call anyway."

In this script, you are opening up — displaying your humanity and vulnerability to your new friend. You've just told him of your hesitation about calling, thus opening the door to real communication between the two of you. If John is at all sensitive, this, in turn, opens the door for him to reveal a bit more about himself. He could possibly respond by saying something like, "I'm really glad you called."

The Ideal Way of Communicating

Because of your goal to get to know John better and to create a bond between you, it's important that you understand the principles of creating a successful conversation. Here are a few that can guide you toward that end.

Open-Ended Questions

One of the best ways to keep a conversation going is by showing interest in the other person. And nothing shows interest in someone else more than asking questions.

153

However, not all questions are created equal. Used properly, questions can display genuine interest. Incorrectly used, they can make you sound like an FBI agent grilling a would-be terrorist. The difference is whether you ask open- or closed-ended questions. Closed-ended questions are like the short questions you used to answer on school tests. For example:

- Where do you live?
- What do you do?
- What kind of car do you drive?
- Do you prefer fish or meat?

Open-ended questions are more like essay questions in that they allow the person who answers to respond in depth. For example:

- What made you decide to move to New York?
- How do you manage your career and be a parent at the same time?
- How do you spend your free time?

As you can see, asking open-ended questions allows you to show interest in John as well as find out a great deal about him.

The following are some terrific open-ended questions that will allow you to find out more about your new friend. But be careful. Some of them should only be asked after you have created quite a bit of rapport and mutual trust.

- If money were no object, what would you do?
- What would your perfect day be like?
- Tell me about some of your goals.
- If you could magically become the historical figure you admire most, who would you be? Why?

- Tell me about your favorite school teacher.
- What's the most fun you've ever had?
- Where in the world would you most like to visit?

As you can see, each one of the answers to these questions can be highly revealing. In addition, each is a bridge to many follow-up questions. After a few rendezvous, you will start to feel comfortable enough to think of all kinds of things to ask. Eventually, you will even get to the point of having fun creating your very own repertoire of thought-provoking questions.

Asking open-ended questions is a wonderful tool as long as they are not too open-ended. If the question is too broad in scope, it can backfire. Here are some examples of questions that are too open-ended:

- How'd it go today?
- What's new?
- What have you been up to lately?
- Tell me about yourself.

Mutual Self-Disclosure

As important a tool as open-ended questions are to the process of fact-finding (one of your goals in meeting John), they do not allow you to reveal yourself. No one can create bonds in a vacuum. Ultimately, you need to reveal yourself in order to create emotional impact between the two of you. The question is, then, "How do I tell him about myself and, at the same time, learn about him?"

The answer lies in the process of mutual self-disclosure. As Alan Garner writes in *Conversationally Speaking* (see Bibliography):

You can promote self-disclosure in your relationships by promoting symmetry. Ask questions, show interest in the responses you receive, and then attempt to link up those responses to your own knowledge and experiences. If the other person is not rude or self-centered, she will probably soon begin asking you questions about your disclosures, too.

Here's an example of how this can work:

Mary: How do you happen to know Ralph?

John: I used to play racquetball with him.

Mary: That's how I met him, too. Although I'm afraid that I don't play very well. Do you play racquetball often?

John: Twice a week or so. Would you like to improve your game?

Mary: Sure. But I'm self-conscious about wasting the time of really good players.

John: In that case, you have nothing to worry about. I'm just an average player who likes to have a good time.

For further in-depth discussion of the art of verbal and non-verbal communication, I recommend that you read *Conversationally Speaking* by Alan Garner (see Bibliography).

A note to men: Until now, I've addressed every aspect of this book equally to both men and women. But the next subject on "closing," while it will be useful to you as well, is particularly important to women. So, my male friends, I ask your indulgence as I speak directly to women on how better to handle guys like you.

The Close

The term, "to close," comes from the world of sales. It is the end game of salesmanship, which is meant to position the buyer toward taking the next step. This principle will help you convert your initial rendezvous into a deepening relationship. Of course, I'm making the assumption that after having spent some time with your rendezvous partner you want to pursue a growing involvement. If that is the case, then I have one bit of advice for you: Learn to close.

Closing, here, means that you don't leave the next rendezvous to chance. So often, women, in particular, become victims of what Erica Abeel calls "Manspeak." Manspeak is equivalent to a businessman telling his unemployed former colleague, "Let's have lunch sometime." It's a polite way to defer making any commitment and is, therefore, next to meaningless. The problem is that on any given night there are millions of single women who are waiting for *the call* from men who have forgotten all about their promise to be in touch. Perhaps women, on the whole, are more literal-minded. They accept verbal commitments at face value. Or perhaps, being more in touch with their feelings, they tend to make promises only when they plan to follow through.

Either way, women do have a problem of losing the initiative. This is compounded by the lingering vestiges of the earlier customs which still make it more "legit" for the man to call the woman. Conclusion: As a woman, you have to fight back. How? By gently committing your new "potential" to another rendezvous right then and there. Don't let him slip out of your life with his trusty (but not so trustworthy), "I'll call you."

Think of yourself as an expert pool player. Do you know the difference between an average and an expert pool player? The intention of the average cue holder is limited to getting the ball into one of the pockets. On the other hand, the expert player has two goals. Yes, he wants to land the ball into the pocket, but he also wants to position himself for the next shot. An expert salesperson does the same thing. Instead of just getting the sale, he positions himself in such a way as to create more sales in the future.

You, too, can be an expert in setting yourself up for the next move by learning to transform your first rendezvous into another one. The key to your success is *timing*.

Timing

Timing is everything. How you control the time elements of your rendezvous will determine the success, or failure, of a potential relationship. Here's how you can make timing work for you: As it does in the theatre, the old adage, "Leave them panting for more," really applies. No matter how terrific your initial meeting is going, avoid allowing the man sitting opposite you to determine its length. If he invites you to have dinner with him and you have an unmistakable mutual attraction, bite your lip and decline. Why? Because you must avoid the "too much, too soon" syndrome, which could overwhelm your fledgling relationship.

Here's an example of an effective way to end the rendezvous. John and Mary are deep in conversation, which has already lasted for forty-five minutes. John is really enjoying Mary's obvious interest in his career. Suddenly, Mary looks at her watch and says, "John, I really have to get going, but I'd love to hear more about your success with the Xerox account. Why don't we have lunch sometime soon?" John, who is just getting into his stride and is definitely stimulated by the conversation, asks, "Gosh, must you leave right now?" Mary nods her head and says, "I'm afraid so. But I really mean it, John, I would like to see you again. In fact, why don't we set up a luncheon for next week?"

Notice how Mary is bowing out at just the right moment — at a time when John is just getting warmed up. Result? John wants more. And because she is the one to terminate the meeting, she is dealing from a position of strength. This allows her to set the terms of the next rendezvous. But that's not all. Notice, also, how Mary displays her listening skills by referring to a specific aspect of John's conversation (the Xerox account). Add to this her warmth and her assertive, professional behavior, and you know that Mary cannot help but win John's respect and, possibly, affection. In fact, he is probably already thinking to himself, "This is no ordinary woman. There's something special about her."

Notice, also, what choice Mary made concerning the location of the next meeting. Instead of an evening date, she proposed getting together for lunch. Why? Because a dinner date could be construed as an invitation to romance. On the other hand, a lunch date, while it is certainly a friendly gesture, still allows both of them to gradually become more at ease with each other.

If getting together for lunch is not your style, another excellent place for a second meeting could be connected to a sport, such as tennis. This kind of encounter is very informal and allows you to share some physical activity together. It's also an excellent way for people who are non-verbal to be able to communicate and share some time without having to sustain long conversations. So, if you both happen to share an interest in some kind of participatory sport, or even jogging or bicycling, you could easily propose that you both wear warm-ups the next time you meet.

Final Compatibility Check

If your rendezvous produced a "potential," you will no doubt feel elated. But before you get further involved, do take the time to compare your new friend's assets against the compatibility profile you wrote out in chapter five. On first impression, which qualities does your POS have that you consider essential? Are there some characteristics that you find unacceptable? Which qualities are negotiable? Which are non-negotiable? Does he/she behave in a manner reminiscent of anyone in your past? If so, was it a positive relationship? Remember, you need never again feel desperate, so don't grab hold of a relationship too fast unless it's really what you want. And for your sake, postpone all fantasies of wedding bells and "happily ever afters" until much later on.

Congratulations! You have now finished the next major part of your campaign. You have used the referral method to meet the "genuine article" — a single POS with whom you share mutual interests. You now know that all the effort you put into the campaign is paying off. And the most exciting thing about this is that you can repeat this process again and again. I hope that you are proud of your accomplishment. You should be. You are winning. Your victory is not based so much on whether you find the love of your life in the first rendezvous or the tenth. What *is* important is that you now own the knowledge of how to repeat this process until you *do* find the love of your life.

Now that you have experienced your first rendezvous, you deserve some fun. No matter what the result, reward yourself for your accomplishment. Do something enjoyable, even outrageous. You deserve it. Celebrating important junctures in your campaign will also give you a sense of the completion of one stage and the encouragement to move on.

The Socially Monogamous

There is much more to be done. First, you need to repeat the process of the referral interview and the rendezvous many more times. This may seem obvious, but it really isn't, especially if your first rendezvous turned out to be a smashing success. You see, at this point, you might be tempted to discontinue your campaign and pin your hopes on this one new relationship. This tendency is quite common among a large number of unmarrieds whom I classify as the socially monogamous.

To find out if you belong to this group, let me ask you this: Do you find it difficult seeing more than one POS at any particular time? If the answer is yes, you must overcome this tendency, at least for the time being. At this point in your campaign, it's essential that you have get-togethers with as many POS as possible. Why? You know the answer. If you see just one new person, you'll feel dependent and lose your initiative. You might even find yourself trying to make an unworkable relationship succeed. (And if you've ever been in a dead-end relationship, you know what a mistake this can be.) Imagine the mental state of an unemployed person going to his only interview for the month and you will picture a desperate person.

The same applies to your campaign. In fact, if you are sincere about finding your mate in the next ninety days, you should set a goal to have at least two new rendezvous a week. Within that time frame, you will have met twenty-four candidates. Of these, unless you are overly critical, you will probably find at least eight to twelve with whom you will strike a chord of mutual interest. Obviously, this does not mean that all eight will turn out to be candidates for a long-term relationship. But a few of them most probably will.

161

You'll then have the pleasant task of choosing between two or more compatible individuals.

The third part of your campaign will consist of nourishing each promising rendezvous toward greater intimacy and mutual discovery. This is the topic of the next chapter.

Chapter Nine

The Campaign: Part III
After the Rendezvous:
Eight Ways to Promote Greater
Intimacy

There is nothing quite like meeting someone special. Suddenly, your every moment fills with the constant awareness of a new presence in your life. Nor is there any mistaking it when it finally happens. After one or several rendezvous, you realize that here is someone you enjoy being with — someone with whom you share much in common. And what's amazing is that just a short time ago, this person who is becoming so important to you was a complete stranger.

Your campaign is succeeding! You are creating new relationships with not only one but, preferably, several POS with whom friendship and even love could develop.

But wait! There is still much to be done. The road from first meeting to permanent love is filled with the remains of half-formed relationships that have gone awry. Obviously, no one can protect himself/herself from the vicissitudes of love. Many relationships cannot survive the close scrutiny that is projected upon them by both partners. Of course, this is not always bad. After all, one purpose for the campaign is to allow you to distinguish between the right and the wrong partner.

But there are also times when a couple who could have developed greater intimacy never quite got there. They somehow let their association flounder and vacillate, almost like a sailboat being tossed about by changing currents. It is this kind of relationship, the one that should have developed and didn't, that I wish to help you save. Here, then, are eight steps you can take to create the atmosphere that will lead to a joyful and ever-growing association between you and a potential mate:

I. Sharing an Adventure

I once asked a happily married couple of thirty-five years what the strongest aspect of their love for each other is. After much thought, the wife replied, "In spite of the many problems in our marriage, the thing that keeps us together is that we share a history. We have gone through so much together that we cannot imagine our lives with anyone else."

Wise words, carrying an important message to you. You see, unless you do something about it, your relationship can fall into a routine soon after it begins: You go out to dinner and a movie, one of you prepares a meal, you watch TV together, and so on. There's nothing wrong with any of these activities. In fact, treated imaginatively, they can be quite wonderful. But if you want to create strong bonds between you, think about spicing your relationship with the kind of fun and adventure that takes a bit more imagination. The more memorable the experiences you share, the more history you build together, the deeper the bonds that will form between you (and the more fun you'll have).

What kinds of activities do I mean? Here are some ideas:

• Physical Activities — There are two good reasons for you to schedule some physical activity as part of the process of getting to know each other. For one, many men tend to experience emotion through physical exertion. In many cases, the closest male friendships are formed as a result of participation in sports together. It's as though physical exertion gives men permission to release and to display their emotional side. A woman who understands this can create good rapport with a man by arranging to do something physically demanding together.

A second reason to do something of a physical nature is that it can allow you to work together as a team. Invariably, when people are involved in a situation where they depend on each other, they create greater appreciation for each other.

You don't have to be a team sports enthusiast to enjoy physical exertion. Frieda, a free-lance writer, invited Alan, her new friend, to join her on a two-day hiking trip. "It was so exciting," she reported. "There we were, just the two of us, having to help each other do everything from reading a map to pitching a tent. In just two days, we grew closer together than we had in the previous six weeks."

Naturally, there are an endless number of ways to share adventures together. You can go biking, take long walks, go swimming in a pond, plant a vegetable garden together, or just play a few rounds of tennis or racquetball. Whatever you do, you'll be creating your own "history" of shared and memorable experiences.

165

• Intellectual/Cultural/Culinary Activities — Not everyone is interested in intellectual and cultural pursuits. However, if you or your friend enjoy such activities, you can create an adventure by attending concerts, performances, and lectures and afterwards, discussing them between the two of you. But don't just choose the same old events. If you are both confirmed jazz lovers, add some spice to your life by attending the opera. It could be the first time you both attend such an affair, which would qualify as a new adventure. And if you both share the same political beliefs, attend a lecture that offers the opposite point of view. See how each one of you reacts. This could make for an unforgettable evening.

Nancy and I have always loved searching for new and different kinds of restaurants. (I especially enjoy it when I discover a terrific "find." I have done it so much in recent years that my friends have labeled me "the sniffer.") We make an adventure of trying all types of cuisine, from Cajun to Hunan. Our attitude is that we'll try anything once. What makes each of these experiences memorable has as much to do with our heightened sense of anticipation as with anything else. Prior to our going out, we like to read to each other the restaurant guide's detailed description of each establishment and its house specialty, delighting in the fact that our imagination is being further stimulated. Once at the restaurant, we sample each new dish with great care, making a point of experiencing every bite to the fullest. Silly, you say? Perhaps. But to us, taking the time to enjoy each moment has given us much pleasure. And in the process, our shared adventures add a new page to our personal history.

II. *Learn about the Other Person's Passion*

Not long ago, I attended a Christmas banquet where I was seated next to a man who started telling me about his wife's passion for travel. "Gwen loves to travel," he said, "but I don't care a thing about it. So every year, she goes gallivanting off with one of her girlfriends. I don't mind, as long as she doesn't want me to go." I must confess to you that I have a hard time with this kind of attitude. That two people would share a life together and not even care to understand the desires and interests of each other is beyond my comprehension.

Do you want to make an impression on your new friend? Then get to know his/her passions. What is the one thing that really interests your friend? Is it work or a particular hobby? Whatever the passion is, get to know as much as you can about it. Nothing creates a nicer impression and is more flattering than your genuine desire to learn about the other person's interests. Even if you feel quite ignorant about the subject, ask questions, and learn as much as you can. What's that you say? You hate football and your friend loves it? Then change your attitude. Get to know the game. As with all things, appreciation increases with understanding. I didn't say that you have to become a pigskin enthusiast. But you can at least present the attitude that if something is vitally important to your mate, then, by definition, it's important to you, too.

III. *Create an Adventure Out of Everyday Events*

There are people who really know how to celebrate life. They can turn the most ordinary chores into little adventures.

It's not so much what they do but how they go about doing it. Let's take, for example, grocery shopping for dinner. Some people can actually transform this ordinary, humdrum activity into great fun. Randy, a forty-one-year-old architect, invited his new friend to prepare dinner with him. They planned the menu together, divided the work between them, and then embarked on a shopping excursion for the various ingredients. "By the time the meal was prepared, we'd already had so much fun that tasting the food was almost an anticlimax," said Randy. "It was a wonderfully memorable evening."

IV. Create a Romantic Evening

Are you a Romantic? Do you enjoy special touches that enhance the love experience? If so, then make this, too, into an adventure. Once your relationship is intimate enough, propose that each of you plans what you consider to be a romantic evening. You can set whatever ground rules you wish, such as the amount of money to be spent, when and where the occasion should take place, and so on. The idea is to allow both of you to express your romanticism.

There are some wonderful benefits to this. First, preparing such an evening will allow you both to display your true feelings for each other. Second, it will add a heightened sense of anticipation to the relationship. And third, it is going to be wonderfully memorable — another bit of happy "history" together.

V. Involve Your Children

Sooner or later, if either one or both of you have children, you'll want to include them in your relationship. Any permanent bond is going to have a major effect on their lives. Conversely, their attitude about the relationship is bound to affect its chances for survival. Therefore, do things together with your friend and your children (and his/her children) that allow all of you to feel comfortable with each other. I realize that in some circumstances this is a tall order. Each family has its own set of challenges to deal with, especially since some children can be resentful of any relationship that involves anyone other than the original parents. But the more you encourage everyone to be involved in projects together, be it sailing a boat or washing the family car, the more the bonds of friendship will grow and the more like a family you'll become.

VI. Talk Out Problems

Arguments, disagreements, hurt feelings — these are all familiar parts of any relationship. Often, people steer away from areas of potential conflict in order to avoid rocking the boat. This is a mistake. No matter how much they have in common, differences of opinion are bound to surface between two people who have their own personality. Think of your disagreements as potential opportunities for growth. Each conflict opens the door to its resolution through the sharing of thoughts and feelings. So, instead of bottling up your emotions, learn to share them with each other.

Nancy and I have adopted the attitude that if we have an argument, we'll try to resolve it before we go to sleep. This way, instead of suppressing our feelings and letting the poisons of resentment fester, we flush them out and replace them with infinitely sweeter feelings of love and understanding. Now I'm not saying that it's always easy to do this. More often than not, in fact, it's Nancy who insists that we "talk it out." (She has taught me, over the course of our married life, that, indeed, this *does* work — even though, in typical male fashion, I initially fought this.) But we have both learned that it's much nicer getting up the next morning, knowing that the hostility of the previous night will have been replaced with feelings of affection. (I seem to recall, however, several times when it took until 4:00 am to accomplish this miraculous change.)

Make a pact with your friend that you will share your feelings honestly with each other. If there is something bothering either one of you, discuss it. Talk it out, find a solution, and diffuse a potential time bomb in your relationship.

VII. Don't "Interpret" Your Relationship

Loneliness and wishful thinking are two powerful enemies to developing greater intimacy. Both reduce our ability to see things as they are. Marilyn is a classic example of this. For the past seven months she has been seeing Blake, a publisher's representative. They have been going out together, on the average, about once every two weeks. For him, the relationship with Marilyn is a casual one. He's dating several women and has no serious thoughts of making a commitment to any of them. But Marilyn, who has experienced much loneliness in her life, has been fantasizing that sooner or later Blake will propose to her. In fact, she has stopped seeing other men, putting all her efforts toward a long-lasting bond with Blake.

This is a scenario for disaster. Nothing can come from this kind of hopeful thinking but pain and disappointment. As your relationship grows, make sure that you assess your mate's commitment to it. If he or she is seeing other POS, you do the same. Furthermore, make sure that the other *knows* about it. If you want to win in love, match but do not exceed the commitment level of your friend.

This kind of attitude is important for two reasons. First, it allows you to display your independence. This is especially significant when dealing with individuals who have difficulty making a commitment to any kind of serious involvement. Second, your continuing your social contacts with others will keep you from feeling a sense of desperation about the relationship. As a result, you will act more naturally, portraying an attitude of independence.

VIII. Toward Becoming "Best Friends"

In interviewing couples who have terrific marriages, I have found one common denominator. They are each other's best friend. Over a period of time, they have developed the kind of trust that allows them to share their innermost thoughts, fears, goals, and aspirations with each other. Of course, this process takes years to mature — you cannot expect to reach such intimacy in a short period of time. Nevertheless, I believe that you can begin to lead a special relationship in this direction from the very start. How? By sharing with each other your feelings about important things. For example, do you know your friend's career goals? Is your friend happy with his/her job? What about you, have you shared your goals and aspirations with him/her? What are some of your friend's dreams? What about yours?

Good friends are able to share with each other the "stuff" of life — the things that make life meaningful. Good friends are also willing to show their vulnerability without fear that at some future date it will be used as a weapon against them. This kind of transparency takes courage. Most of us are afraid of being hurt again. Yet, I promise you that if you are willing to risk opening up, you will help your friend to open up also.

In *The Friendship Factor* (see Bibliography), Alan Loy McGinnis tells about a famous psychiatrist who boasts about his ability to have his patients reveal quite a bit of themselves from the very first session. His method? With each new patient, he shares something of an intimate nature about himself. Now, I am not recommending that you tell everything there is to tell about yourself indiscriminately to everyone. But if in the process of getting to know a new person you learn to share bits and pieces of your inner self —perhaps a fear that you have or a minor failing — you will open up the possibility for your friend to respond in kind. This helps to create an atmosphere that allows true friendship and caring to grow.

As you can see, there is much that you can do to keep your relationship growing. Naturally, to make any of this work, you must have the cooperation of the other person. He or she must be as enthusiastic about your association as you are. But assuming that you both care for each other, you can gradually steer your relationship toward greater intimacy by incorporating the principles outlined here. After all, that's what this campaign is all about: to help you find your soul mate — someone you care about who also wants to form a growing and deepening bond with you.

Chapter Ten

I Will . . . Until

You *know* what you want! A special person with whom you can share your most intimate secrets — someone who understands you and loves you just as you are. You want to experience the joy of anticipation when you know that your loved one is coming home and the simple pleasures of sitting at the kitchen table on a blustery, rainy Saturday morning, both of you in your bathrobes, sipping a steaming cup of coffee and reading the paper. You want to be able to share your successes and setbacks with someone who cares deeply. You want to know that you have a soul mate, someone who sees the world as you do. You want to make love the way people do who have nothing to conceal from each other — openly, joyously, and yet familiarly. You want to find someone with whom you can share the bittersweet experience of gracefully growing old together. You want never to be lonely again!

I don't know if I have evoked the images of love that speak to you. I can only draw on my own experiences and values. What *is* important, my friend, is that you realize at all times what it is that you are working for. Why? Because along the way, you will be tempted to shift from the high activity level of a ninety-day campaign to a less committed effort. It is simply human nature to lose interest in projects that do not yield immediate results. This is precisely what you must guard against. It is an inescapable truth that those who win in anything important have developed the ability to make a commitment and stick to it.

I call this the "I will . . . until" principle. This principle simply states that you will persist with your campaign until you achieve your desired result: find the love of your life. The key to this philosophy is rooted in accepting reality. People who practice it do not have a Pollyanna outlook; they do not expect everything to go smoothly for them. In fact, they are completely familiar with Murphy's famous law, "If anything can go wrong, it will." They know that as they embark on their campaign all sorts of things are bound to go wrong.

What then, keeps these people going? Is there a secret antidote to feeling discouraged? Yes, there is, and those who succeed in their campaign know what it is: They are aware at all times of *why* they're putting forth the effort. To them, the trade-off is clear. They compare the rewards of love and companionship against the effort required to achieve them. And because they focus on the desired results, these winners are able to motivate themselves to make the next phone call, set up another referral interview, and plan another rendezvous.

In order for you to succeed in your search to find the love of your life, you, too, must decide to persist through whatever obstacles will undoubtedly come your way. And I can assure you there will be plenty of those little devils to contend with.

What kinds of obstacles? Just the normal disappointments that are part of any attempt to make something happen. For instance, if you set up a referral interview and end up receiving no assistance, set up another one and keep going. If a POS "no shows" to an appointment you scheduled, don't get discouraged, just keep going. If it looks as though you met someone special and that person, for some reason, doesn't feel the same "spark," call someone else and keep going. If, as a result of unexpected obligations, you discover that you have less time for your campaign than you initially expected, then adjust your plans (only if you must) but definitely keep going. *The key is to keep going.*

To keep your motivation high, hold fast to those images that symbolize permanent love and visualize them as clearly and as often as you can. For many, writing their goals down and reading them every day helps. Others prefer affirming what they want verbally. Whatever works for you, do it. And keep going.

Time Commitment

The most important decision you need to make is to devote enough time to your campaign to make it productive. How much is enough time? As much as you can spare! By thrusting yourself as soon as possible into a high activity level, you can create an extraordinary amount of momentum. And once you have momentum, everything becomes so much easier. For example, it takes tremendous initial effort to overcome one's inertia and actually get up from the easy chair, walk over to the telephone, conquer the inevitable nervousness that accompanies the fear of the unknown, and call a new referral. But once you make the first phone call, it's considerably easier to make the second and easier still to make the third. In addition, once you are in full swing meeting lots of new people, you become more self-assured and, therefore, less dependent emotionally on the reactions of any one person. In other words, momentum can help you create an attitude of confidence, an air of independence — a most attractive quality. (A friend of mine, a woman who makes a point of dating lots of men, describes this as an I-care-but-I-don't-care attitude.)

I am keenly aware of the fact that each of you has a different time problem. Some of you are hard-working executives with very little spare time except on weekends. Some are single working parents with pressing responsibilities. And some of you may be entrepreneurs who work at your business from morning until late at night. I fully realize how much your time is at a premium. So let's discuss time, beginning with the assumption that you have little of it to spare.

Regardless of how busy you are, you, like the rest of us, have some unproductive time. (Even though you may insist that you don't.) All of us waste time. As preoccupied as you may be, you *do* spend *some* time in an unfocused manner: watching TV, reading the newspaper, or doing something else of a low-priority nature. That's why, in order to use your time more productively, you must use a calendar. At the beginning of each week, fill in all your important obligations, such as working, studying, shopping, and anything else that you must do for yourself. If you have children, don't forget to schedule in their activities. This can include having a family night and any other quality time you set aside for them. In addition, pencil in whatever other responsibilities you have which you consider important. After you do this, look at the time you have left. Devote the rest of it to your campaign. Be creative. For example, you can always meet people for an early-morning breakfast or during your lunch hour. If your late evenings are busy, what about right after work? Dedicate every available slot of time to your campaign. Next, schedule the various activities of your campaign such as phone calling, referral interviews, and rendezvous into the available openings on your calendar. The resulting plan should now constitute your weekly activities.

It may well be that your present social involvements can also be used to your advantage. But take a look at them from the vantage point of your having a goal. For example, if you are involved in a singles club at your church and you are meeting new people there, that's great. But if your social life consists of playing poker with the boys or bridge with the girls, you may need to reevaluate your priorities to create time for your campaign.

Developing a Support System

By definition, human beings are social animals. Why else would we spend time searching for a mate? Most of us do not enjoy doing things alone. We like to feel the support and encouragement of others. We also like feedback to make sure that what we're doing is working. Receiving outside encouragement in order to achieve a personal goal definitely works. That's why people attend such organizations as Weight Watchers, Alcoholics Anonymous, and the like. By involving others and enlisting their support, you can avoid becoming like the little steam engine that tried to make it uphill all by itself but, instead, chugged down slowly to a dead halt. Besides, doing something important and knowing that others are cheering you on adds a dimension of fun and excitement.

What kind of support can you get? There are several options:

• Get a buddy. The buddy system is one of the most

effective ways for you to get support. A buddy is a person who is experiencing the same things you are. In this case, your buddy would be another single who also wants to follow the steps of the ninety-day program. Because both of you make the commitment, you now have someone with whom to relate. You can agree to monitor each other's activities and to be (lovingly) strict in case one of you "weakens" and does not accomplish as much as had been planned. In addition, you can set special times to make phone calls together. Each person can listen to the conversation of the other on an extension phone and offer feedback and helpful suggestions.

Ideally, a buddy is there to cheer you on when you are winning, to encourage you when you need a pep talk, or (when necessary) to aim carefully when you need a gentle boot in the derriere. But there is a caveat: Sometimes, "buddy" programs turn sour. This happens when either party begins to seek sympathy instead of encouragement. So, if you choose one, make sure that your buddy is as committed to the end result as you are.

Another way to use the buddy system is to create a group of several friends to go on the campaign together. You can rotate buddies and meet weekly to account for each of your activities. If you want to be really creative, you can even devise a goal sheet and give points to each of the activities described in the campaign. For example, you can give points for setting up referral interviews, for each new name that you receive from a referral interview, for having a rendezvous with a POS, and so on. If you are really adventurous, you can even pool your funds and give a prize to the person who puts forth the greatest effort. This is an excellent way to create additional motivation and, most important, to introduce an element of fun to the whole process.

There are lots of variations to this. I'm sure that with creativity you can come up with all kinds of original and motivational ideas with your friends. The key is to do whatever you have to do to keep going.

• Elicit the help of family and friends. Suppose you don't have a buddy, can you still find the support you want? Of course you can. You can ask your family and friends. I hope that by now you have overcome at least some of your reluctance to let others know of your desire to find your ideal mate. A family member or a trusted friend can be wonderfully supportive of your campaign. This is what you should do: Out of your inner circle of close friends and relatives, choose one person whom you feel you can take into your confidence. Explain to that person what you're doing and what your activity goals are on a weekly basis. Tell him/her that you simply need someone to help monitor your progress and that you would like to schedule an unbreakable date to meet weekly for the next twelve weeks. At each meeting (which shouldn't last more than twenty to thirty minutes), you'll want to discuss your weekly activities and compare them to the goals you set for yourself. This really works, because it makes you accountable to someone else. In the case of the businesswoman I described in chapter two, her support came from her two teenage children. They understood how easily she could be distracted by her business activities. And because they love her, they wanted her to find companionship. "I couldn't stop the program even if I'd wanted to," she later told me, smiling. "They were so insistent that I follow through that I felt like I was the teenager and they were my parents. But it was wonderful. Without their support, I doubt if I ever would have gotten started."

So get the help you need, if you need it. There's no reason for you to have to "go it alone" with your campaign, just as there's no reason for you to have to go it alone in life. Whether it's a buddy, a family member, your minister or rabbi, your therapist, or your favorite professor, get the help you need, but most important, *keep going*.

Chapter Eleven

Men, Love, and Sex

———————◆———————

This chapter is about men and how women should learn to deal with them. I decided to write about this because men, far from being the strong sex, are an emotionally fragile lot, especially when it comes to love. As a result, they tend to be afraid of deep emotional attachments. They wreak havoc with their relationships with women — particularly those that evolve into a growing commitment — leaving their female counterparts confused, hurt, and angry. Because this widespread tendency to resist love is not fully understood, many potentially viable relationships — those that could have had a chance to succeed — fail.

In my research for this book, I ran across many women who have become "gun-shy," reluctant to venture into yet another temporary liaison with a man. How can you blame them when, time after time, an apparently loving man would abruptly cool off, and, on one pretext or another, end the relationship and disappear?

In writing on this subject, I profess no Olympian objectivity. My comments will cut a wide swath across Adam's descendants. However, they are based upon endless discussions of this topic with both men and women, on the eloquent writings of others, and, finally, on an understanding of my own maleness.

Should you think that I view myself as an exception to the rule of innate female emotional supremacy, you would be mistaken. On the contrary, I am prototypical of the all too common problem many men have in forming lasting relationships. To illustrate this, let me tell you about my own pre-marital relationship with Nancy.

As I look back on our two-and-a-half-year courtship, I marvel in complete gratitude at the way Nancy handled our relationship. And although I loved her immensely, I am not sure if, left to my own devices, we would be married today (or if I would be married to anyone, for that matter).

Our "affaire d'coeur" began on the fourth floor of the College-Conservatory of Music in Cincinnati where students sharpen their musical skills in little cubicles known as practice rooms. We had noticed each other before, but it was during one of the periodic breaks we both took to assault the ubiquitous vending machine that we actually began to chat with each other. Our talk ranged from opera, which Nancy was studying, to our favorite restaurants (a motley lot, as I recall, controlled, as it were, by our meager student budgets). It was clear that we were both enjoying our time together. In the ensuing weeks, our practice breaks became longer, a circumstance that became evident in our respective lessons. But our relationship flourished, as we would find more excuses to spend time together.

One evening, I invited Nancy to join me for a chamber music recital by the LaSalle Quartet (our first "date"). Since both of us had to take a music history exam the following morning, Nancy invited me afterwards to study with her at her off-campus apartment. I'm not sure how much studying we did, but the privacy of Nancy's apartment allowed us to demonstrate our deepening affection for each other. Four days later, Nancy invited me to a private dinner of homemade French cooking.

During this time, I was becoming increasingly smitten with Nancy. And with my growing attraction to her, I felt as if I were losing control. This filled me with panic. Just a month earlier, I had terminated a rather "sticky" affair with a woman who had kept repeating that she would do "anything for me" if I would marry her. (I never knew what "anything" meant.) As a result of this unhappy relationship, I had promised myself, during the remainder of the time that I was pursuing my studies, to avoid any relationship that went beyond "fun and games." But then, I had not counted on meeting Nancy.

After the perfectly romantic French meal at Chez Nancy — replete with pouton au gratin, peas sauteed in sherry, and mousse au chocolate — followed by an exquisite evening of tenderness, I felt compelled to assert my independence. Looking serious, I said, "Nancy, there's something I have to warn you about". . . (Dramatic pause). . . "*Don't* fall in love with me." I was certainly not prepared for her response. Being sufficiently self-possessed to handle such hubris, she looked directly at me in complete disdain and replied, "Apparently, Ben, you don't know me very well," whereupon she got up from the sofa, picked up a stray cup of coffee, and confidently walked into the kitchen, the revolving door swinging behind her.

I was put in my place, for sure. But I was also fascinated and, yes, charmed. Here was a woman who was putting up with none of my nonsense. (Much later on in our courtship, after we had both professed our love for each other, Nancy confided that she, even before that fateful evening at her apartment, had already known that she was in love with me. In fact, she went on to reveal, she had known for several weeks that I was "her man." But she was smart enough to realize that if she had let me know her true feelings in that early and very tentative stage of our relationship that I would have been, most assuredly, scared away.)

Nancy understood that I, like so many men, was afraid of intimacy (a fact of which, at the time, I was completely unaware). How she had gathered this knowledge at such a young age, I do not know. But she instinctively realized that a relationship built on love and mutual respect would depend on her always dealing from a position of strength. From the moment she rebuffed my pompous comment, I knew that I was involved with someone who would not tolerate being treated as an inferior. And although I was already highly infatuated, it was then that I understood why she was the first woman who had ever truly captivated me. (Later on, I learned about the long thread of female independence in Nancy's stock. Her mother, a devout Christian, had insisted that the preacher strike the word "obey" from her marriage vows. And her maternal grandmother divorced her second husband while in her late sixties on the grounds of "incompatibility.")

For the next five months, the two of us remained inseparable. But not once did either of us mention the word love. Nancy was not about to crowd me in. She made sure that our relationship deepened to the right degree. One night, feeling closer than ever, I turned to her and said, "I know we promised to keep our relationship free of serious feelings, but I can no longer keep it to myself. . . I love you." Wearing a pained expression, Nancy inhaled deeply and sighed. Her eyes glistened as she said, "I've wanted to say that, too, for a long time now. . . I love *you*." Embracing her with all the tenderness I was feeling, I must have repeated over and over again those three simple words.

Two years later, we were talking about marriage. Because of our studies, we ended up in two different schools for one year. At the end of that year, we both knew that weekend bus rides between Bloomington, Indiana, and Cincinnati, Ohio, and endless long-distance phone conversations were not adequate substitutes for being together. We decided to get married.

As soon as I made the commitment to marriage, I began feeling anxious again. I started thinking that maybe I couldn't handle it — maybe I wasn't meant to get married, ever. I became moody, irritable, taciturn. Nancy noticed my changed behavior. Finally, she insisted on knowing what was bothering me, so I told her.

"All right, let's discuss this," she said to me with slight impatience. "For one whole year we've been separated from each other. You had opportunities to break away. So did I. We didn't because no one else interested us. Unless we make a commitment, the alternative is that I stay at Indiana University and you remain in Cincinnati. Is that what you want?" Of course I didn't want that. "Look, darling," she continued more softly, "I know that we are taking a risk. But at least we know how happy we are together." Then with a brilliant close, she concluded, "Neither one of us likes it the way it is now. We've known each other for over two years —long enough to know what we want. Don't you agree?"

Nancy understood that, like her, I, too, was "hooked." At this point, she realized that she had to take the initiative and force me to make a decision. But she only took that liberty when our relationship was at its ripest — not before. Four months later, we got married. That was in 1972. Our marriage has grown and blossomed ever since.

I tell you this story for several reasons: first, to show you how Nancy, by exercising sensitivity to my all-too-male fears yet still dealing from a position of equality and assertiveness, deftly negotiated two crucial junctures in our relationship, thus allowing it to grow — second, to let you know how much I found her assertiveness appealing. With Nancy, there was and still is the silent understanding that our relationship must be based on mutual self-respect. She would no more accept my taking her for granted today than she would have when we first met. Because of this, we, to this day, still court each other.

The third reason I write about this is because so many women have had relationships with men that went nowhere. I have talked with women who are afraid of developing any attachment to men. Several have had "close calls" — marriages that almost happened where the man backed out at the last minute. "What's the matter with men, anyway?" was the question put to me by a charming interior designer in her early thirties. "They seem so contradictory. Sometimes they can show so much affection. At other times, they want to be distant. I always feel like I'm walking on eggshells, never knowing where I stand."

What is the problem with men? Why do they seem to have so much difficulty with love and marriage? It seems that a more-or-less universal male fear in our western society is the fear of losing control. Men, on the whole, are not very aware of their emotions. Once they create a certain order in their lives, through their work or out of habit, they tend to stay on that course even if something is missing. Emotions are held at bay as they focus their attention on competitive achievement through work or recreation. When a strong emotional impact is created by another person, as in a budding relationship, many men, according to Dr. Rollo May, begin to fear "being totally absorbed by the other, the fear of losing one's self and one's autonomy."

This is the kind of feeling that I must have experienced when I "warned" Nancy, "Don't fall in love with me." It may have come across as arrogance, but, in retrospect, it was more of a plea for help. I was unable to cope with the depth of my emotions. Had she acted insecurely, Nancy would have tried to "make me" love her, or, as had happened in my previous relationship, tried to pressure me into a greater level of commitment. That would have had the opposite effect. I would have probably panicked and evanesced like a Monterey mist in the morning sun.

Curiously, once a woman penetrates her mate's wall of resistance and he falls deeply in love with her, the fear of losing control resurfaces. This time, it is caused by his need to resist the overwhelming pull to become emotionally dependent on her. When men fall in love, they fall hard. This is especially true when they fall in love for the first time. Since they have never experienced this onrush of deep feelings for a woman, they are emotional virgins. As a result, they fear drowning in this new whirlpool of emotions. Some become "clutchy," attempting to possess the one they love. This, in time, kills love. (As I write this, I'm listening to the Metropolitan Opera's broadcast of Verdi's *Otello*, surely the most vivid and poignant example of obsessive love carried to extreme.) Other men, fearing they will lose their identity, simply back off. This becomes especially evident at major turning points in a relationship, such as when a couple talks of marriage or when the woman becomes pregnant —events that symbolize a growing commitment to the relationship.

Fortunately, not all men suffer from these fears to the same degree. Some are secure enough to not feel out of control. Others learn to overcome their fears. Still others, particularly those who have been married before, have dealt with these feelings previously and may now be eager to create a new bond with a compatible mate. (Most divorced men remarry within two years.)

If you are a man and you have noticed in your past relationships a tendency to retreat as soon as you begin to experience feelings of love or to become critical of your mate when she needs more commitment from you, then you are probably dealing with a bout of the fear of losing control. Seeking "the perfect woman" and, therefore, always finding fault with every female you meet is yet another way this fear may be manifesting itself in you. If any of this applies, you need to understand your destructive behavior and harness it so that it will not sabotage your chance for love. I also recommend that you read *The Six Demons of Love, Men's Fear of Intimacy* by Steve Berman (see Bibliography).

How to Deal with Men

As a woman, you need to understand how much stronger your emotional foundation is in most relationships. Learn to understand men's fears and to not take their fearful behavior personally. This will prevent you from acting defensively.

Not all men can be helped by you. Should you find that you are dealing with an extreme case of a man who is so afraid of intimacy or who is becoming too possessive and yet is unwilling to face his "demons," then you may well have to look elsewhere.

So, here you are, yearning for permanence, filled with a desire for love, ready for a man to love you and with whom you can start to build a future, and you are faced with men who either are afraid of falling in love or who, as often happens with much older men, want to possess you. And you say, "It isn't fair." No, it isn't. But then, who ever promised you that life is fair? Forget about fairness, and steel yourself with the determination to help a potentially wonderful mate overcome his resistances and become the love of your life.

Sex and Your Campaign

For many singles today, sex has become the routine ending of an evening out. Whether out of a sense of loneliness, social pressure, or desire, for some the sex act has become the predictable finale to any date, the contemporary surrogate of the good night kiss.

Some of these attitudes are changing. A recent full-page ad for a new book proclaimed: "The 'Sexual Revolution' is over and the 'Age of Commitment' has just begun." It seems that as people seek permanence in their relationships, they are finding it increasingly difficult to separate sex from love, as was the habit in the sixties and seventies. There is a growing awareness that, as progressive as we like to think we are, indiscriminate sex is somehow counterproductive to developing growing commitments.

The problem is that, in the face of changing attitudes, few people know how to behave. If the pendulum is swinging away from casual sex, is it swinging back to a world of stifled sexual urges and double standards? Are we simply experiencing a reactionary movement toward Victorianism? Fortunately not. With all its excesses, the ferocity of the sexual revolution was necessary to confront the vestiges of restrictive attitudes about love and sex that made the lives of countless individuals a private hell. Today we can discuss sex and love openly, thus helping millions better understand life's central forces.

Nothing illustrates more convincingly the beneficial effects of our changing attitudes than seeing Barbara Walters discussing male impotence on national TV with couples who are dealing with this problem. That a woman can lead such a discussion so central to men's greatest sexual fear in front of millions of viewers is an astounding example of the progress we have made. It seems that, after all, the pendulum isn't swinging back. Instead, we are part of an evolutionary continuum that is moving toward a greater integration of love and sex.

This integration also means that sex does not have to be treated as casually as sneezing. It means that in your relationships with POS sex should be a part of a growing level of intimacy. Therefore, those who use sex as an introductory act may be short-circuiting the process of "peeling the onion" that allows for a relationship to move naturally from one step to the other.

In subtle ways, your attitude about sex will change once you decide that you want to be on a campaign to find permanent love. Your goals are now long term, not short term. Perhaps, in the past, you went to bed with someone whenever you had a sexual craving. Now, you need to view your behavior in terms of developing a long-term relationship. With that in mind, here is a general principle for you to ponder: Having sex before you have developed a level of caring and intimacy can hurt a budding relationship more than it can help. In talking with many single women, this view has been confirmed. The consensus has been that the occurrence of sexual relations before men and women really get to know each other usually truncates the process of developing intimacy.

Sex can be viewed in two ways. It is either a mere release to a strong biological urge or, without negating the power of the sex drive, it is the ultimate way of expressing a growing intimacy between two people. Viewed the first way, sex is a disjointed action between two individuals who use each other for their own needs. This often curtails the chance for a deepening relationship primarily because it is manipulative. On the other hand, sex as the ultimate expression of intimacy is a natural progression of the growing bond between two people. In your campaign, understanding the difference between the two can be crucial to your developing a long-lasting relationship.

Don't misunderstand what I'm saying. There is no set time frame before which it's not okay to have sex and after which it becomes all right. There are times when men and women develop tremendous closeness within a short period of time. At other times, the bonding process takes longer. But if you view sex as a natural extension of your communication of true affection, you will always know when the time is right to unleash its wonderful power of expression.

Chapter Twelve

Variations of the Campaign: How to Use What You've Learned in New Ways

———◆———

By learning the methods in this book, you have acquired a great deal of practical information — information that should help you be much more in control of every aspect of the mating game. Besides applying what you've learned to the campaign itself, you can also use it every time you run across an opportunity to meet new people. For example, if you happen to be sitting next to an interesting POS on an airplane, you can now use the interview techniques you've learned to become better acquainted with your seat partner. Or, should you meet a PSS in an activity unrelated to your campaign, you might make a point of exchanging names of POS. My point is that you should not isolate what you've learned by applying it solely to the campaign itself. Instead, use its methods in every creative way available to you.

Below, I've outlined some new ways that you can apply what you've learned. These are not meant to supplant the campaign itself. Nothing is as effective as meeting people one-to-one through the method it describes. Nevertheless, for those of you who like variety, here are just a few of the many ways you can apply the techniques outlined in this book:

Blind Dates

The blind date is a much-maligned way for people to meet each other, and yet it has been responsible for many marriages. (My wife's parents met on a blind date, and I would say that their relationship was a pretty good one; they were happily married for over forty-five years.) Although not as much in vogue as it used to be, the blind date does offer an opportunity of spending some time in a socially acceptable setting with an otherwise unknown POS. Curiously, these dates are not as "blind" as one would think. In most cases, the POS involved will be someone with an area of mutual interest or common socio-economic background. Ultimately, the reason blind dates occasionally work is that your friends are likely to "fix you up" with someone they think you might like.

Am I suggesting that you seek this kind of date? Not at all. It's still not nearly as effective as conducting your own campaign. But if the opportunity arises and someone invites you to go on a blind date, don't be too hasty to decline. It may be worth the gamble.

Dinner Parties and Other Arranged Introductions

Rudy and Marcie are an extremely happy couple. They are having the time of their lives traveling across the United States together. And yet, only six months before, Marcie, recently widowed after thirty-five years of marriage, was so depressed that she was contemplating suicide. What happened? Rudy and Marcie were both invited to a bridge party by mutual friends who thought they would enjoy each other's company. "At first, I wanted to scream," Marcie told me as she recalled that evening. "I had been so wrapped up with my loss that I couldn't even think of seeing a man." But gradually, with Rudy's patient persistence, Marcie started going out and having an increasingly more wonderful time.

Little dinner invitations by friends can lead to finding someone special. After all, your friends do know you, and they also know the other person.

Of course, there are some disadvantages. For one, you are stuck for the evening. In case your partner is a bore, there is little you can do except wait it out. You also have to protect your hosts' (it's usually a couple) feelings because they might feel guilty if the match doesn't work out. Therefore, you should take great pains to make your hosts feel good about their support. Reassure them of your appreciation for their efforts, no matter what happens. This way they will be encouraged to invite you again.

Classes, Courses, and Seminars

Without a doubt, our colleges and universities are among the most fertile mating grounds around. In fact, before the reorientation of sexist attitudes in the late '60s and '70s, many women grew up believing that college was the place to find a husband. I am not sure to what degree this still exists, but I would wager that even today, among a significant minority, this attitude still predominates.

Today, thousands of older singles are returning to education as a tool to meet their counterparts. Adult education courses, both on and off campus, are burgeoning as more single adults partake of courses ranging from assertiveness training to wok cooking.

From the point of view of the campaign, attending classes is an excellent way to meet others. This is particularly true of courses which last over a period of several sessions and where class participation is encouraged. There, you are able to develop the kind of familiarity that leads to trust. Over a period of a few sessions, everyone in the class recognizes each other sufficiently to become comfortable talking among themselves. And if, indeed, you are studying a subject that genuinely intrigues you, you are meeting fellow classmates who also share your same interests.

Of course, there are also a few disadvantages to signing up for a class. First, it costs money to attend. Second, you may not find anyone who appeals to you. These disadvantages disappear, however, if your interest in the course itself is the primary reason for attending. In that case, your new knowledge will make you a more interesting person in general, whether you meet a POS as a result of the class or at some future date.

Groups, Associations, and Clubs

Jayne, at thirty-six, a brilliant vice-president of a computer marketing company in Silicon Valley, was extremely happy with her life — with one exception. Although she had no difficulty in meeting men, she found that most became intimidated as soon as they learned the extent of her success. Finally, she hit upon a plan. Researching the clubs and associations in her area, she joined the most exclusive ones — the ones where she felt she could find men who were at her success level and above. Next, she made a point of meeting with the president of each of the associations and asking him to "take her under his wing" and introduce her to other singles. In addition to the country club and a sports club, Jayne decided to also learn flying, another activity which attracts high achievers. As a result of all these efforts, she is now enjoying a very satisfying relationship with Steven, an entrepreneur who is stimulated, not intimidated, by her achievements.

Joining active organizations can be productive. Sometimes. The difference between a good experience and a waste of time depends on you. Here is how to make joining an organization more productive:

1. Research. There are thousands of organizations reaching almost every segment of the population. Before choosing one, investigate it to make sure that it will be both enjoyable and worth your time. For example, singles clubs are not necessarily more conducive to your meeting POS. Often, they tend to inhibit relationships. One woman told me that in her church's singles group, which consists of several hundred members, there are few romances. It seems that everyone is having such a good time socializing together that there's a reluctance for the members to start romantic entanglements lest it might somehow interfere with the camaraderie of the group. On the other hand, Jerry, an Air Force civilian, joined the Public Relations Roundtable in his city. Although his job was marginally involved in PR, his research indicated that the club was predominantly female. Since he was attracted to career women, the fact that many of these women were go-getters was an added plus.

2. Secure an introduction. Even when you join an association, it's an excellent idea to deal from a

197

position of strength. Most associations are always looking for new members, and, therefore, your interest in joining will always be welcomed. However, because you want to meet eligible POS, it's an excellent idea to have a respected ally within the organization. Here's what you can do: Find out who the president of the group is and call him/her. Explain that you are interested in finding out more about the organization. Would he/she be open (familiar terminology?) to getting together informally to discuss your membership in the group? Most likely, the president will be delighted. After all, as a leader, the president likes to sponsor new members into the group. When you get together, express your genuine interest in the club. But also ask to be introduced to other singles whom the president thinks you would enjoy meeting. Now you have an ally who will introduce you to PSS and POS, thus helping you in your campaign.

The 20/20 Party

Carolyn Kellams, who teaches relationships classes in the San Francisco area, told me of a group of women who found a creative solution to a social problem. San Francisco is not an easy place for a woman to be single. With a huge homosexual population, it can be quite discouraging for a woman to allow herself to become attracted to a man. She never quite knows if she's wasting her time or not. To solve this problem, a group of twenty women decided to throw a party. To ensure success, they made the following stipulations:

- Every woman had to bring one male friend with whom she was not presently involved.

- All the men had to be heterosexual.
- All the men had to be single.

After giving assignments for everyone to bring wine and hors d'oeuvres, a location was chosen in a beautiful Bay Area setting. The party turned out to be a huge success. In fact, since then the group has grown considerably.

You can create the same kind of "share the wealth" party with your friends. Only one suggestion: Have the men bring the hors d'oeuvres. In the San Francisco experiment, this was a rousing success because the men outdid the women in displaying their culinary creativity.

For the "Higher Purpose" Person

I know that some of my readers are going to have difficulty doing things for themselves. No matter how logical the argument about their deserving happiness, these kind souls can only acquire a sense of purpose in their lives by helping others. They embody the volunteer spirit that makes for the army of people who gives its services freely to society.

Are you that kind of person? Then perhaps you are having difficulty launching a campaign that is focused on helping yourself. I have already offered you many convincing reasons why you need and deserve to go on a campaign. But instead of trying to change you, let's see if we can combine your philanthropy with your personal desire for a compatible mate. By all means, find a project to sink your teeth into. By all means, develop a sense of purpose in your life. Just don't forget about your needs as well.

Find a project you believe in, but also make sure that it will allow you to meet POS. Are you a divorced father? Then do as Terry did. He didn't just join the PTA, he got involved. By becoming active, he had a chance to meet all the new members. Do you live near an Army base or in a big city?

Then do as Theresa did. She volunteered her efforts to the USO. With her open, friendly manner, she was able to meet many single, lonely men on an informal basis. Do you enjoy the arts? Then do as Betty did. She decided to join her city's symphony orchestra young professional group. But instead of just going, she became an active participant. She's the one who pours the wine at the party. As a result, she gets to meet everyone. These are just examples of ways you can get involved that will make you a part of a group, thus allowing you to meet people in a personal way.

Serendipity

There is an unusual word in English. It's called "serendipity" — the ability to discover good things by accident. It's a bit like being able to attract good luck. Ever notice how some people have all the luck? How they seem to pluck the fruits of success out of trees you didn't even know existed? Well, the campaign can make you very lucky in your love relationships. How? Because of your activity level.

Think of it! You are meeting a growing number of single people. Some become friends and acquaintances. Others become more than that. You have told quite a few people that you are in the process of expanding your horizons. Now you are involved in a whirlwind of social activities. Sure, sometimes you get discouraged. That's understandable. But something magical is also happening. Through your constant involvement with people, you are becoming more outgoing, more self-assured and at ease with people. That makes you very "attract"-ive.

Having interviewed so many, you are developing powerful communication skills and a growing ease in dealing with all kinds of people. Now, when you are on an elevator or in the supermarket and you see someone who interests you, instead of feeling too shy, you say "Hello." You find yourself in total control of the situation. You start a conversation, exchange phone numbers, and follow up with an invitation to have "a cup of coffee and a chat," and voila, you're on your way

Could all of this have happened to you without your having launched a campaign? Theoretically, yes. People do meet each other by accident. But, practically speaking, these "chance encounters" can be viewed as a wonderful serendipity — a result of the high activity level of your campaign. You are now more than ever aware of your self-worth; you have visualized your ideal partner; you have acquired skills in talking with people; and, most of all, you have reduced your feelings of anxiety by learning to deal with POS from a position of strength. You are no longer desperate. You're at ease, well-practiced in the art of building a relationship. Now, when a chance encounter comes your way, you know what to do. You are as natural and as comfortable as a Barry Bonds catching a fly ball in Candlestick Park.

I want to urge you to embark on your own ninety-day campaign as soon as possible. Don't let complacency set in Keep your eyes on your goal at all times, and you will be rewarded with the fulfillment and happiness that come from finding the love of your life.

Before We Say Goodbye . . .

Let me share with you a few parting thoughts. First, I want you to know and believe that regardless of your history, your hurts, or your disappointments, you *can* find the love of your life. There are far too many lonely people in this world who have given up on finding companionship. You don't have to be among them. After reading this book, you have all the knowledge you need to find your mate. There are no excuses for you to remain alone unless, of course, that's what you really want.

Second, promise yourself to do more than just read this book. Even if you're not ready for the concentrated ninety-day program, choose an activity level that you can live with. Break it down to weekly goals: How many referral interviews are you going to have in a week? How many rendezvous? . . . and so on.

Finally, I want you to know that I care about your success. Write to me and let me know how you're doing with your campaign. Keep me informed of your progress and any new ways you've discovered to use these techniques. And in case you're getting married as a result of your campaign, by all means, send me a wedding invitation!

Here's to you and *THE LOVE OF YOUR LIFE*!

About the Author

It is the view of Ben Dominitz that only those with a broad range of experience and perspectives can hope to understand today's complex challenges. His life exemplifies this Renaissance approach.

Trained as a concert violinist and conductor at Juilliard and the University of Cincinnati, Ben entered the business world as a way of seeking financial independence and, while in his twenties, developed a successful sales training company offering instruction to thousands of men and women. To further broaden his experience in human motivation, he also did extensive research and consulting in the field of career counseling.

In 1984, he wrote *TRAVEL FREE! How To Start and Succeed in Your Own Travel Consultant Business* ($19.95, Prima Publishing), the first book on the field of outside sales in the travel business, now in its sixth printing. This was the first book published by Prima, which he owns with his wife Nancy. Today, Prima is one of the largest independent publishing companies in the United States.

Bibliography

Works Quoted in this Book:

Bach, Dr. George R., and Deutsch, Ronald M., *Pairing: How to Achieve Genuine Intimacy* (New York, NY: Wyden, 1970). Appearing on p. 13 of the Avon paperback edition.

Branden, Nathaniel, *The Psychology of Romantic Love* (New York, NY: Tarcher, 1980). Appearing on p. 97 of the Bantam paperback edition.

Garner, Alan, *Conversationally Speaking* (Los Angeles, CA: Psychology Research Associates, 1980). p. 60.

Giblin, Les, *How to Have Confidence and Power in Dealing with People* (Englewood Cliffs, NJ: 1956). p. xix.

Morris, Desmond, *Intimate Behaviour* (New York, NY: Random House, 1971). p. 75.

Packard, Vance, *The Sexual Wilderness* (New York, NY: David McKay, 1968). p. 205.

Schnall, Maxine, *Every Woman Can Be Adored* (New York, NY: Coward, 1984). p. 76.

Spake, Amanda, "The Choices that Brought Me Here," *MS.* magazine, November, 1984, p. 138.

Viorst, Judith, "To Be or Not to Be . . . Beautiful," *Redbook*, August, 1976, p. 190.

Works Referred to but Not Quoted in this Book:

Berman, Steve, *The Six Demons of Love* (New York, NY: McGraw-Hill, 1984).

Bolles, Richard Nelson, *What Color is Your Parachute?* (Berkeley, CA: Ten Speed Press, 1984).

Frankl, Viktor E., *Man's Search for Meaning* (New York, NY: Pocket Books, 1963).

Geeting, Baxter and Corinne, *How to Listen Assertively* (San Francisco, CA: International Society of General Semantics, 1976).

Maltz, Maxwell, *Psychocybernetics* (Los Angeles, CA: Wilshire Book Company).

McGinnis, Alan Loy, *The Friendship Factor* (Minneapolis, MN: Augsburg, 1979).

Newman, James W., *Release Your Brakes* (New York, NY: Warner Books, 1977).

Swell, Lila, *Success, You Can Make It Happen* (New York, NY: Jove-HBJ, 1976)

Other Recommended Books:

DeAngelis, Barbara, Ph.D., *Are You The One For Me?* (New York, NY: Delacorte Press, 1992).

Godek, Gregory J.P., *1001 Ways To Be Romantic* (Montebello, CA: Casa Blanca Press, 1993).

Gray, John, Ph.D., *Men Are From Mars, Women Are From Venus: A Practical Guide for Improving Communication & Getting What You Want in Your Relationships* (New York, NY: HarperCollins, 1992).

Hendrix, Harville, Ph.D., *Getting The Love You Want: A Guide For Couples* (New York, NY: Harper Perennial, 1990).

Hendrix, Harville, Ph.D., *Keeping The Love You Find* (New York, NY: Pocket Books, 1992).

Kelly, Mary Olsen and Don, *Finding Each Other* (New York, NY: Simon & Schuster, 1992).

General Index

How to Romance the Woman You Love—The Way She Wants You To!

Lucy Sanna with Kathy Miller

U.S. $12.00 paperback/$14.95 hardcover
Can. $16.95 paperback/$19.95 hardcover

Find out what women really want in a relationship. The authors share the results of their nationwide survey and reveal women's most intimate desires. This book includes dozens of stimulating strategies and imaginative suggestions to help fulfill the potential of a first date, or renew the passion in a lifelong love. Your partner will find you irresistible!

How to Romance the Man You Love—The Way He Wants You To!

Lucy Sanna

U.S. $12.00 paperback/$14.95 hardcover
Can. $16.95 paperback/$19.95 hardcover

"A guide for romancing men by a woman who *really* understands them."
—John Gray, Ph.D., author of *Men Are from Mars, Women Are from Venus*

Rekindle his passion for romance, and learn the truth about what he finds utterly irresistible! Men from all over America reveal their secret soft spots, and all the little things that make them find some women irresistible.

To Order Books

Please send me the following items:

Quantity	Title	Unit Price	Total
_____	_____	$ _____	$ _____
_____	_____	$ _____	$ _____
_____	_____	$ _____	$ _____
_____	_____	$ _____	$ _____
_____	_____	$ _____	$ _____

Shipping and Handling Depend on Subtotal	
Subtotal	**Shipping/Handling**
$0.00–$14.99	$3.00
$15.00–$29.99	$4.00
$30.00–$49.99	$6.00
$50.00–$99.99	$10.00
$100.00–$199.99	$13.50
$200.00+	Call for Quote

Foreign and all Priority Request orders:
Call Order Entry department
for price quote at 916/632-4400

This chart represents the total retail price of books only
(before applicable discounts are taken).

Subtotal $ _____

Deduct 10% when ordering 3-5 books $ _____

7.25% Sales Tax (CA only) $ _____

8.25% Sales Tax (TN only) $ _____

5.0% Sales Tax (MD and IN only) $ _____

Shipping and Handling* $ _____

Total Order $ _____

By Telephone: With MC or Visa, call 800-632-8676, 916-632-4400. Mon-Fri, 8:30-4:30.
WWW {http://www.primapublishing.com}

Orders Placed Via Internet E-mail {sales@primapub.com}
By Mail: Just fill out the information below and send with your remittance to:

Prima Publishing
P.O. Box 1260BK
Rocklin, CA 95677

My name is _____

I live at _____

City_____ State_____ Zip_____

MC/Visa#_____ Exp. _____

Check/Money Order enclosed for $ _____ Payable to Prima Publishing

Daytime Telephone_____

Signature_____